Cat Thao Nguyen is an Australian writer and lawyer. She was born in Thailand to Vietnamese parents and grew up in Western Sydney. Cat Thao is married to Tony, a Canadian Chinese man whom she met at a sushi bar in Vietnam. She has dabbled in filmmaking and theatre but unfortunately has never played the violin or piano. Cat Thao has keen interests in creative arts, economics and the leadership role of women in emerging economies like Vietnam. She is particularly passionate about quality fish sauce and Australian shiraz.

WE are HERE

CAT THAO NGUYEN

ALLEN&UNWIN
SYDNEY · MELBOURNE · AUCKLAND · LONDON

First published in 2015

  This project has been assisted by the Australian Government through the Australia Council, its arts funding and advisory board.

Australian Government

Australia Council for the Arts

Allen & Unwin
83 Alexander Street
Crows Nest NSW 2065
Australia
Phone: (61 2) 8425 0100
Email: info@allenandunwin.com
Web: www.allenandunwin.com

Cataloguing-in-Publication details are available
from the National Library of Australia
www.trove.nla.gov.au

ISBN 978 1 74331 927 7

Internal design by Lisa White
Set in 11/17 pt Minion Pro by Bookhouse, Sydney
Printed and bound in Australia by Griffin Press

10 9 8 7 6 5 4 3 2 1

MIX
Paper from
responsible sources
FSC
www.fsc.org   FSC® C009448

The paper in this book is FSC® certified. FSC® promotes environmentally responsible, socially beneficial and economically viable management of the world's forests.

To Mum and Dad, my heroes.

Công cha như núi Thái Sơn
Nghĩa mẹ như nước trong nguồn chảy ra.
Một lòng thờ mẹ kính cha,
Cho tròn chữ hiếu mới là đạo con.
Ngày nào con bé cỏn con
Bây giờ con đã lớn khôn thế này.
Cơm cha, áo mẹ, công thầy,
Lo sao cho đáng những ngày ước mong.

CHAPTER 1

Ten taels of gold

I was born, two months premature, in a former prison. Sikhiu refugee camp was on the Thai side of the Thai–Cambodian border. At the time, the world only knew of people fleeing Vietnam by boat. My family had travelled by foot.

In 1969 President Nixon began the first modest withdrawal of US forces which had been fighting to prevent South Vietnam from takeover by the Communist North. The South struggled on with depleted resources while the North Vietnamese advanced steadily over the next few years towards the South Vietnamese capital, Saigon. Through March and April 1975 remaining American military and civilian personnel were evacuated. On 30 April 1975, Saigon finally fell. The iconic images of a North Vietnamese tank storming the gates of the revered Presidential Palace demonstrated unequivocal defeat. A mass exodus of

South Vietnamese refugees through the late 1970s and early 1980s followed. The world watched the images of countless crammed boats perilously leaving the shores of Vietnam, drifting haphazardly throughout the South China Sea. For some of the escapees, destiny led them to islands like Pulau Bidong off the Malaysian peninsula and to refugee camps in Thailand. Some would make it as far as America, Canada and Europe; others, crammed like animals into boats that were barely seaworthy, falling victim to pirates, disease or starvation, wouldn't make it at all. Within four years of the end of the war, my own family would embark upon an exodus from Vietnam—a similarly treacherous journey.

•

My family is from the rural district of Gò Dầu in the southeast province of Tây Ninh, approximately sixty kilometres northwest of Saigon (now known as Ho Chi Minh City). The district is only ten kilometres from the Mộc Bài border crossing between Vietnam and Cambodia. The province is bordered by Cambodia on three sides.

My father's father was a successful businessman and his family was one of the first in Tây Ninh province to own an automobile—an imported European car. He was a solemn, hard-working man with a deep sense of pride. Many people in Gò Dầu still recall his integrity and work ethic. He passed away when my father was just a young man. I have only ever seen one photo of him. It sits on the ancestral altar in my parents' house. I can recognise my father's enquiring eyes in the black and white image of my grandfather.

My mother's family was much poorer than my father's. They lived in a small hamlet on land that had been in my maternal grandmother's family for generations. On this land, large clusters of bamboo grew and children played in safety among the burial places of ancestors surrounded by coconut and durian trees.

In the 1950s, during the French colonial rule of Vietnam, several forces emerged. Cao Đài is a religion born of Tây Ninh province and blends Buddhist, Christian and Confucian thought. At the time, it had its own army of soldiers headquartered in the Cao Đài Holy See in Tây Ninh. They were known as French sympathisers. The Việt Minh was an anti-French group fighting for independence that later, after the withdrawal of the French, evolved into what became the anti-American, pro-Communist Việt Cộng. The Cao Đài and Việt Minh soldiers were the only Vietnamese forces in the South who were armed with guns and other weaponry. During the day, my mother's family, like many others, were terrorised by the French, who accused the villagers of harbouring anti-colonists. It was not uncommon for rogue soldiers from either the Việt Minh or Cao Đài army to rob and beat them at night. The family would hide their money in the treetops using tall bamboo stalks and routinely survey the premises. But despite their efforts, they consistently fell victim to abuse and exploitation. Like many others, they were humble civilians governed by fear.

My maternal grandfather was angered by the visible injustices of being ruled by white men. He became a passionate French resistance activist, leading a group of young revolutionaries. As an unusually tall man with a fierce commanding presence, he was a natural leader. But his activities increased the family's adversity. He was repeatedly arrested and tortured. With each arrest, my grandmother had to procure loans in order to pay bribes to secure her husband's release. Such consistent disruption was the reason why my mother's family was less well off than my father's. The family was in constant debt yet, despite this, my mother's parents ensured that all their children were educated. They believed freedom and independence could not be achieved without literacy. Opportunity could not blossom without education.

According to my mother, my father was known as a man with a high level of self-respect. Others called it arrogance, accusing him of being an intellectual snob. He kept to himself, immersed in the study of literature, history and French. He was particularly fond of the play *Les Misérables*. As a teenager, he moved to the central highland province of Lâm Đồng, four hundred kilometres from Tây Ninh, to attend a special agricultural high school. As a young student he cherished the few international colour periodicals the school was able to obtain. He fondly remembers sitting in the library as the periodicals were removed from glass cabinets. Under strict supervision, he gently turned and caressed each page of text and each image, indulging in his deep affection for literature. He was a reflective young man, always deep in thought, in marked contrast to his confident and extroverted younger brother. Though my father studied agricultural production, he had a strong inclination for scholarship, particularly arts and literature. After graduating from high school in 1966, my father moved to Saigon to do an extra year of study in agricultural production before enrolment at university. He specialised in forest management and went on internships throughout Southern Vietnam, studying the effects of mangrove and acacia plantations on soil erosion.

Throughout this time, the Vietnam War was raging. In 1968, both sides agreed to a two-day ceasefire during the sacred Lunar New Year celebrations of Tết. Nonetheless, the Northern Communist forces launched a surprise attack on 30 January 1968, the first day of Tết. The bloody attacks on military and civilian command centres were subsequently known as the Tết Offensive. In the aftermath of the attack, South Vietnamese president Nguyễn Văn Thiệu imposed conscription to increase the resources of the South. Most able-bodied men were required to participate in the war efforts. All those who were uneducated or couldn't bribe their way into higher, safer positions were sent to the front line. Many did not return.

That same year, my young introspective father joined the military as a lieutenant in the Transportation Artillery Unit. Though my mother's family was not very well off, her family was well connected. Her uncle was deputy director of prosecutions in the South Vietnamese justice system. Another uncle was a colonel who travelled in his own helicopter and was never without an entourage of guards. Thanks to these connections, my mother's brothers were made captains and lieutenants in the police force, postings that kept them safe from the front line, far from the deafening booms of gunfire and bombs. The insignia on their uniforms indicated their rank. Women looked yearningly upon them with adulation as the men walked the streets with glowing pride, collecting pockets of admiration.

Meanwhile, the North was faring well in the war of propaganda, inspiring a loyal following among poor peasants in the South who were disillusioned with their own poverty and drawn in by Communist ideals of classlessness and shared ownership of land. In an effort to recapture the devotion of the peasantry, in 1970 President Thiệu announced a land reform initiative. Under the program, the government would purchase unused or abandoned private property and use existing state holdings to grant land to peasants. Low-interest loans would be issued to these new landowners to start their agricultural businesses. The program required capable and knowledgeable people to assist in its administration. In 1973, my father passed the required exam to become one of two officers in the Mekong Delta province of Cần Thơ to assess and approve these microfinance loans. He was then permitted to leave his position in the military.

For two years, until the fall of Saigon, my father visited small villages and spoke to peasants about their business plans. He talked to them about rice seeds, fertiliser, animals and machinery. At the time, there was a new breed of rice that was ready for harvest only three months after planting. It was known as the rice from the heavens. The land reform program was successful and brought prosperity to many. Amid a persistent war, my father provided hope for countless poverty-stricken families to carve out a better life. He understood how a simple official signature could radically shift the fate of weather-beaten men and women who lived in unremarkable mud huts. Desperation came in the form of bribes and while others were tempted, my father never took a single cent. He embraced his responsibility with objective fairness: signs of a principled and courageous man who frequently witnessed how lives were transformed before his very eyes.

And still the war kept on. It was a time of uplifting war songs, when girls fell in love with uniformed men, and American products and lifestyles were imported into South Vietnam. Concurrently, images of the horror and bloodiness of the war and the bodies of American soldiers were beamed into the living rooms of American families. Anti-war protests ensued around the world. Diplomats met, bombs dropped, journalists wrote and people continued to die.

My mother had moved to Saigon to study law. She lived in a small haunted house in District 4. At night, as she climbed into the wooden loft to sleep, she would hear the scraping of furniture as the souls of agitated dead soldiers meandered below. Not far from the house was a small canal where occasionally bodies would be found drifting.

The screams of destruction and the scent of death continued for a few more years until North Vietnamese forces stormed into

Saigon to capture the city on 30 April 1975. North Vietnamese tanks rolled down the main boulevards, past the lounge bars the American GIs had frequented. Việt Cộng soldiers, previously in hiding in the South, appeared suddenly in full public view, marching through the streets. My mother watched as people, driven by panic, began to run. She didn't know where they were going but they just ran in a wave of deranged and violent hysteria. South Vietnamese soldiers dumped their weapons in the canal near my mother's house and stripped themselves of evidence that they were associated with the fallen regime, for fear of the coming retribution. Some decided it was smarter to immediately join the North Vietnamese forces on the day of the fall of Saigon. These became known as 30 April soldiers. But for many, this act and any other futile attempts to hide their poisoned history would not save them.

My father was at work when Saigon fell. In the office, his colleagues were overwhelmed with fear as they began to under-stand the ramifications. They were right to be afraid; in the months and years following the fall of Saigon, those associated with the former regime were punished and persecuted. Decorated soldiers, diplomats and government officials of the South were decried as enemies and traitors of the new Vietnam. People's courts tried class enemies. Land and assets were seized and redistributed. The rise of the proletariat crystallised. Farmers became landowners and gardeners became governors. Việt Cộng who had lived secretly in and around the Americans and the soldiers of the South emerged brazen and bold. They were neighbours, school teachers and family members. Government and private offices were taken over.

My father's sister's rice-husking mill was appropriated by newly appointed Communist officials who had until recently been uneducated peasants. They moved into her house and publicly denounced her as a rotten capitalist in a type of people's 'court' at a gathering of local villagers. Although she was known to be kind and fair in her business dealings, those who did not denounce her as a traitor were viewed with suspicion. If she had mistreated anyone she ever dealt with, this became a trial of revenge. At the insistence of the officials overseeing the hearing, some villagers reluctantly came forward to condemn her. But despite the possible retribution, others came to her defence. Similar scenes played out around the country, though the former workers and farmers who became powerful government officers were not always as forgiving as those who had previously been powerless and now revelled in a new world order.

My father was ordered to continue to work. He sat there idly as the Việt Cộng tried to implement tasks in the transition to Communism. Immediately, the old unacceptable money bearing the Southern Republic's imprints had to be changed. My father watched as people came in and out of the office to change their money. He was constantly harassed and interrogated by his new bosses, seeking intelligence about people he knew. *Where are they? What are they doing? Who are they related to?* The harassment escalated as the Communist officers became increasingly paranoid about secret assemblies of resistance.

Eventually my father was sent to a re-education camp; the higher the rank, the longer the sentence. My father was imprisoned for two years, while my uncles who had been captains were held for ten years. The camps were designed to punish, humiliate and decisively break men who were seen as traitors for siding with foreign oppressors. Their purpose was to introduce the men to the notions of Communism and assimilate them. On a few occasions my maternal grandfather made the long trek north to visit my uncles at the camp near the Chinese border. They were barely skin and bone, forced to eat only what they could catch: rats, cockroaches and lizards. They were *ngụy*, filthy people who had betrayed their country.

At the time, my father's family still had hidden wealth. They pulled together sufficient money to bribe officials to release him. While physically he'd survived his two years of imprisonment, the horrific experience would forever change him. I have never learned the details of what happened to him during that time, and I have understood never to ask.

Meanwhile, all the males in my mother's family except for her father and her youngest brother, who was only fourteen years old, were imprisoned in re-education camps. Their lineage meant harsh persecution by the new authorities. Within a short period of time, the four remaining children—the three eldest of whom were daughters—were charged with the family's survival. The hardships they experienced in the early years after the war are almost unfathomable. For example, the three sisters shared one pair of pants between them and therefore only one of them could leave the house at a time. This sole pair of pants was patched again and again and again in a ridiculous ensemble of brokenness.

As the implementation of Communist reforms gathered momentum, almost everything was controlled and rationed by the government. The production, supply and movement of commodities were strictly monitored. Official government outlets were set up to trade approved goods. Trade outside government channels was prohibited given that, now in the new Vietnam, private enterprise was illegal. Each individual was permitted to purchase rations of essentials. Registered households with proper documentation accounting for each individual in the residence were permitted to pool their rations. Every month, families, clutching their residence registration documents, would line up outside government warehouses to purchase small quotas of essentials, such as sugar, salt, rice and MSG. There were severe shortages and often after lining up for hours there were no products left to purchase. Naturally, a black market emerged.

My mother, with her entrepreneurial and audacious spirit, decided to trade in unrationed produce. Goods could not be transported outside a delineated area of production. What was produced in Gò Dầu had to remain in Gò Dầu. This included meat and rice. With unrationed raw pork tied to her belly underneath her clothes, she would ride the buses that ran between Gò Dầu and Saigon, where she sold the meat to black market vendors in the city at higher prices than those set by the government. She became known to the drivers and the bus inspectors on key routes, and they offered her sympathy and protection. (According to my aunt, being a pretty unmarried girl in her early twenties didn't hurt; that rule is the same everywhere!) After she handed over the meat trade to her sisters, my mother moved into operating an illegal rice trade. At night, the rice farmers would hide in the darkness in small boats on the river. From the back of her house along the riverbank, my mother would keep a lookout. When it seemed safe, she would light a lamp as a signal. The boat would quickly emerge from the darkness, and head towards the shore to deliver the rice to her for distribution. It was a risky exercise, each and every time, an uncertain dance of luck and danger, as capture would have meant imprisonment.

On one occasion, she lit the lamp as usual. The river was still and she waited for the black patch to take shape before her. The nearby bridge was quiet as curfew was still in place. But suddenly, from the shadows, she heard: 'I've got you!' She withdrew quickly into the unlit house, frozen with terror, unable to breathe. She listened in the placid darkness to the conversation between the rice farmer and his captor. The captor was just a civilian, but someone who had aligned himself with the new regime. The police were called and the farmer was imprisoned. Knowing the police would interrogate the farmer, demanding to know the name of his accomplice, my mother left immediately for Bien Hoa province to visit one of her brothers who had been moved to another re-education camp. Her father was working several kilometres away in the family's rice fields, which had been taken over by the state. He travelled out from the fields to join her in Bien Hoa, but they decided not to stay overnight as they usually did on their visits for fear that the farmer would betray my mother to the authorities, who would then come for her sisters back home. My mother eventually discovered that the farmer was held for a long time. He was brutally bashed but he never disclosed her identity. The integrity and courage of this ordinary man would stay with her, to surface in unexpected moments when she was an older woman, standing in an unassuming kitchen in Sydney or while she waited to pick up her small children from school—it would call to her like valiant drumbeats from a distant past.

Despite the incident, my mother continued her black market trade. While her older brothers were detained indefinitely in re-education camps, as the eldest in the family she was responsible for her three younger siblings. She existed like a wounded animal, near death, moving on instinct and desperation. At night, she boarded small trucks to take the bags of rice from Gò Dầu to central Tây Ninh, passing various checkpoints. Again in a dance with danger. The script was set. The characters knew their roles and their lines. Finally, the enterprise fell into a routine rhythm. The nimble impulses of survival again found a way. For some time she succeeded, passing through various checkpoints unhindered, but inevitably there came a day when she was stopped by an inspector.

She approached the checkpoint. My mother tried to look nonchalantly sombre—a look that many of the other tired travellers wore. But the man stopped her and she was inspected. The other passengers watched in silence as she dropped to the ground and cowered on all fours, begging them like a slave child for lenience. *Forgive me for being poor, kind sirs.* The salty warm tears of shame and anger rolled down her cheeks. She stared at the boots in front of her, refusing to meet the eyes of her new masters. Finally, she was permitted to leave but her precious contraband was taken. It was yet another wrenching setback.

My mother moved on to another initiative. Taking the family's entire savings, she decided to go to Saigon to buy contraband coffee and other items to bring back and sell in Tây Ninh. But as she was walking through the city to meet the trader, she was pushed to the ground and robbed. All the family's cash was gone in one decisive stroke. My mother could not fathom facing her family. There was nothing left. She stood there, her patched pants mocking her. The usual chaos swirled around her as she contemplated the classroom she used to sit in not long ago. The slow despair crept inside her bones. She was twenty-two years old. A hummingbird inside an engulfing storm cloud that devoured her. She wanted to stop flapping. She wanted to stop fighting. No more white noise. No more guessing. No more frightening episodes of army boots approaching, crawling for safety at night and scrambling for shreds of life in the day. For a long time, overwhelmed by defeat, she thought about the nectar of death. How peaceful it would be. Its seduction lingered on and my mother struggled to resist. But the faint lining of consciousness came back. A forced rational reality interrupted her thoughts, demanding her to come back to her family. She eventually awoke to the stark knowledge that her family needed her. She made her way back home.

Not long after, my mother's tenacious will to live returned. She decided to trade trash. Bottles, duck feathers, tin cans, pieces of board, steel—for anything reusable, there was a buyer. But capital was required. My mother took the clock from the wall, the radio, the rice cooker, tables, chairs and lights, and sold them. She pawned my grandfather's ring numerous times. Like many Vietnamese women, my grandmother had a solid jade bangle. Jade is precious, and once you put a jade bangle on your wrist you are never meant to remove it because it has protective powers. As it is meant to sit snugly around a woman's wrist, it is shatteringly painful to put on but even more excruciating to take off. My grandmother's jade bangle was the last reminder of better times. As my mother soaped her mother's hand, she pulled violently at the bangle until bruises swelled and hand bones neared breaking point. They sat on the floor of the wooden house, now empty of belongings and quickly filling with storylines of vast sadness. The river looked on in curious quiet. As they held the soaped jade, both women wept through throbbing pain and splintering heartache.

With the money she had amassed, my mother gathered together a group of family, friends and villagers and gave each a little bit of money to source goods. They would reassemble with a collection of trash, which she would on-sell to a distributor. But some of the desperate women took the money and never came back. When my mother went to collect it, she found them starving. She not only forgave the debt but bought them rice. It was another failed venture that stabbed brutally at her.

In an emerging empire of ruthless savagery, her kindness was her downfall. Her sweet student disposition could not compete against the torrential hustle of this new reality.

With what little money she had left, she set up a small packaging operation. Under the new Communist regime, all books and documents related to the old South Vietnamese government had to be destroyed. History was to be rewritten. Street names were to be changed. My mother went to schools and purchased their history books, geography books and any other books that contained unpermitted knowledge. She then set up a production line of neighbourhood kids who cut and glued the paper into foldable bags of various sizes and sold them to market vendors who had not yet been stopped by the authorities for trading outside the system. The vendor would fill the 100-gram, 200-gram and 500-gram bags with sugar, rice and other products. At the same time, she regularly went to Black Lady Mountain, thirty kilometres away, to buy custard apples to distribute to children to sell on buses and at bus stations. The kids would each carry a tub of heavy custard apples, weaving in and out of the buses like swift hungry mosquitoes. Each child bulging with wit, tragedy and grime.

•

When my father was released from the re-education camp in 1977, he returned to the small village just outside Gò Dầu where he had spent his childhood. He soon realised that my mother was one of the few educated women left of marriageable age and a similar class, and he decided he would marry her. It was not an extensive courtship and there wasn't anything romantic about it. A week after they met, my mother accepted my father's proposal because he fulfilled her two conditions—he was educated and he was not disabled from the war.

They were married on 16 November 1977, two and a half years after the war ended. My father and my mother each had toiled through their own traumatic episodes. Each soundlessly suffering, forcefully containing it within.

My mother borrowed a wedding dress from one of her sisters-in-law. My father slit the throats of his family ducks, de-feathered them and helped to cook his own wedding feast. My mother's father borrowed money from relatives in order to host the celebration. At the wedding, they were given just enough money by the guests to pay back the loans. There wasn't even enough left over to make a pair of pants. Looking at my parents' black and white wedding photos, I'm struck by the lingering sadness they exude. My mother is smiling in only one of the pictures; at the prompting of the photographer, she is feeding my father cake. She wore the only pair of shoes she had—tired old black sandals. A portrait shot of her illuminates her beautiful features, reminiscent of a French–Vietnamese blend. But enduring melancholy seems permanently trapped in her eyes. She was a young girl becoming a woman in postwar Vietnam, too often tarnished and defeated with no one to hold her. She stares at the camera—demure, on the brink of a future so terrifyingly uncertain.

Not long after the wedding, the river began to swell like the belly of a malnourished child. It was a cruel bash at open wounds of a village trying to simply stay alive. The flood engulfed the market a hundred and fifty metres from the riverbank. My mother's belly was swollen too; she was about to give birth to her first child. She slept on two beds stacked one on top of the other, elevated above the water's flow, gritting her teeth in silent, excruciating pain. A son was born and she clutched him in her arms as the bitter, pernicious flood forged on.

After the birth, my mother stayed with her parents so they could help look after her and the baby. They could not afford for everyone to eat rice so while my nursing mother ate rice, everyone else lived on cassava roots. My father went to work on my late grandfather's pepper plantation, trying to remain inconspicuous. He rarely went to the central part of the village for fear of identification and further persecution by the authorities. My father never spoke of his time in the re-education camp to anyone, not even my mother, choosing instead to submerge the memories in drink, often in the company of peers whose life had taken a similar turn. Discarded men who were draped with the same cloak of disillusionment. Once the proud son of a well-to-do businessman, dressed in crisply ironed shirts, he now found himself with a small baby, living off the proceeds of his labour on the pepper plantation. The rice wine soothed his nightmares and eased his fears.

Not long after, rumours circulated around the village that the authorities were searching for my father. The authorities had determined that, without any training or equipment, he was going to be assigned to de-mine fields ridden with landmines. The news shook him deeply. Tremors of dread burrowed their way into his marrow and began to consume him. For many years, despite a changed reality, the dread would stay with him. He knew that death was upon them. When my father told my mother, she looked at him. He was not just her husband, the result of a hasty marriage: he was now also the father of her son. She made a choice. All around her, men of the former southern regime continued to be persecuted and they each began a slow death as indignity decayed them. She could see no future for their family here. In 1979, my parents decided to leave Vietnam.

Living as they did in a landlocked province, they had no access to a boat. For them, the quickest way to get out of Vietnam was through Cambodia. My mother's family had a friend who agreed to smuggle them across the border. Mr Tỷ was my grandfather's god-brother and a trusted family friend; he was like an uncle to my mother. He was the only reason they decided to leave via that route and at that time. They paid him ten taels of gold upfront, which was an incredible amount at that time; today it would be close to A$17,000. Many families could never imagine obtaining such an amount of money in their lifetimes.

Mr Tỷ hired various smugglers to take my family through Cambodia all the way to Thailand. In the group to leave was my mother, father, twelve-month-old brother, fifteen-year-old cousin and fifteen-year-old uncle. Each smuggler would take them to a certain rendezvous point and there hand them over to the next person. By then, the Khmer Rouge, under the dictator Pol Pot, had been ravaging Cambodia for four years from 1975, ultimately committing genocide. More than two million Cambodians perished in the name of his futile attempt at social re-engineering towards an agrarian-based Communist society. All those suspected of being educated were slaughtered. These included people who wore glasses, indicating they were able to read. Mass graves with severed heads and limbs were later found, as were the graves of babies who had been smashed against trees in order to save bullets. The site of these graves would later become known as the Killing Fields. The mania of Pol Pot was stopped only when the newly unified Vietnamese forces invaded Cambodia in 1979 to oust the Khmer Rouge. Within Cambodia, Vietnamese refugees were fleeing the new Vietnamese government, Khmer Rouge soldiers were fleeing the Vietnamese forces and there were random paramilitary Thai soldiers lining that country's border with Cambodia. Refugees were also being kidnapped and traded to international humanitarian organisations in return for bags of rice.

In this time and place of utter madness and amid this terror, my parents embarked on their exodus through Cambodia. Later, reports would state that as many as half of all those who left Vietnam by boat died. But out of every four people who tried to flee Vietnam over the Mộc Bài border into Cambodia, three were shot. Later still, some researchers estimated that only ten per cent of those who undertook this journey by foot survived.

CHAPTER 2

A simple sarong

In the middle of the night in late 1979, my mother sat silently, steeped in sorrow, in the house where she had given birth to her son and before the ancestral altar where she had been married. The flood waters had long receded and the river was calm. Her mother, father, sisters and youngest brother wept in silence for fear the neighbours would guess my parents' intentions and inform the authorities. No one could be trusted and everyone wanted to appear to be supporters of the new Communist officials so betrayal by neighbours was not uncommon. Her two sisters held her tightly, sobbing violently into their hands cupped against their mouths in the pitch-dark. There was no way of knowing whether the group would survive the journey ahead of them. My mother's lips trembled.

The next day, they left the only world they had ever known, uncertain of when and if they would ever return. The carnage, trauma and pain of the journey would be inconceivable.

•

It was late in the afternoon during the wet season. The rice crop was almost ready to be harvested. It was unsafe to travel all together, especially with a woman and baby. At the time, most of the refugees, particularly those who travelled by foot, were men who left alone. My father took his nephew, Hải, and my mother's brother, Hồng Khanh – both fifteen – to the Mộc Bài border crossing. Posing as merchants, they arranged for bicycle taxis to take them to the Cambodia border town of Bavet. Traders frequently crossed the border, and they were not questioned. They stayed overnight in Bavet with a smuggler, waiting for my mother.

Late that night, my mother, holding her baby, moved through the rice fields which lined the road to and beyond the border. She was accompanied by one of the men Mr Tỷ had contracted. It was rough terrain, often with no clear path. The border was heavily guarded with armed guerrillas on both sides. Close to the border, my mother tripped and fell into a small ditch. Immediately she clamped her hand across my brother Văn's face as he struggled to cry out.

Someone yelled into the darkness. 'Who's that?! Who's there?!' *Bang, bang, bang.* The frighteningly rapid thunder of gunshots punctured the air. Paralysed with fear, they huddled in silence, my mother trying to soothe her baby. Strangely and fortunately, as if aware of the danger they were in, Văn was quickly compliant and placid, like an old man with deep knowing trapped inside a baby's body. They stayed crouched in the vast and empty rice fields for a long time until the night was silent once more. Eventually they continued walking, arriving scared but safe in Bavet, at a small hiding spot where they met up with my father. The next day, my mother's father crossed the border on a motorbike and met them to say goodbye to his first daughter and youngest son one last time. My grandfather looked long and hard at his son. He observed with pride that Hồng Khanh was tall, highly intelligent and mature for his age. He was sure to survive the journey, he thought. He did not know that this was to be the last time they would ever see each other.

Led by the smuggler, the small group made their way to a large provincial town where they took a ferry across the Mekong River to the busy city of Neak Luong on the other side. They boarded the ferry together with motorbikes, trucks, bicycles, beggars and animals. Once on the other side, they went into hiding, waiting for the smugglers who would take them on the next stage of the journey to Phnom Penh, the capital of Cambodia. In the late afternoons, my father would walk by the river, watching as people washed and small children played in naked innocence, oblivious to the monstrous atrocities plaguing their country. One afternoon my father found a French dictionary, titled *Larousse*, discarded on the side of the road. He found it so strange that it lay there so passively, so unwontedly. Something that he would have nurtured like a sacred relic. He quickly picked it up and took it back to their hiding spot. Inside the book was a map of Cambodia. As he studied it, he realised how far away from the Thai border they were. The realisation devastated him. But, he reminded himself, when they'd made the decision to leave Cambodia, they had knowingly chosen to risk death rather than face what life held for them in Vietnam. Despite the dangers, they would have to keep going, wherever fate would lead them. There was no turning back.

After ten days or so in Neak Luong, they made contact with the new smugglers, who took them by bicycle to Phnom Penh, approximately sixty kilometres away. Once they arrived in the capital, the hungry, tired fugitives and their weak baby hid in the roof space of a small house. In the early hours of the next morning, they set off for the provincial town of Battambang, the second most populous city in Cambodia after Phnom Penh, three hundred kilometres away. They followed the national highway by foot and at night slept hidden in the shadows by the roadside. Along the way, my father saw many European cars—Peugeots, Renaults and Mercedes—abandoned by the side of the road. Chaos had descended upon Cambodia under the Khmer Rouge regime. Anyone caught in possession of a luxury vehicle—a sure sign of a capitalist—was likely to be butchered by the Khmer Rouge.

One night, as they were preparing to sleep on the roadside, my father walked away from the group in order to go to the toilet. To his surprise, he came across a manufacturing facility which was heavily guarded by Vietnamese forces and allied

Cambodian soldiers. It looked as though this was some sort of checkpoint. The factory appeared to be newly built and bore the logo of Blackstone. My father knew of the company because his sister had had a Blackstone diesel engine in her rice-husking mill. The sight of the familiar logo brought his family sharply to mind and all at once he missed them so much his body ached. He knew that his departure would mean trouble for them with the authorities.

Days turned into nights, comprising a series of anxious hours until they finally arrived at Battambang. From there they travelled along the railway towards the town of Sisophon. Like Vietnam, Cambodia too had been colonised by the French, and between 1930 and 1940 the French had built a railway from Phnom Penh to Poipet on the Thai border. From Battambang, there was a single-track line. People travelled along the railway on a single flat panel made of bamboo and attached to wheels; it was moved along manually with a type of pump. If there was an oncoming traveller, everyone would gather their belongings and lift the wheeled panel off the rails. This method was used to transport animals, people and produce. As the smugglers got the contraption ready, my family sat in a nearby field among some cattle, eating a small ration of food.

Finally they arrived at the town of Sisophon, roughly fifty kilometres from the Thai border. There they hid in a tailor's house until the smuggler could arrange for another four people and bicycles to take them further. The gentle old Cambodian tailor gave my mother a mandarin. It was almost completely dried but had enough juice left to give to my brother Văn. A little juice and vitamin C was a luxury that he sucked on ferociously. The old man's kind presence radiated humanity. 'Go to Thailand?' the tailor asked in Cambodian. My father understood the word Siam and indicated that they were. The old man looked at the baby boy gnawing the fruit and smiled. This simple generous gesture from a gracious stranger would forever embed itself in my father's memory. He would later reflect that it could have been this little drop of juice that separated Văn from life and death.

This moment of humanity soon dissipated when the smuggler demanded money from my parents, declaring that Mr Tỷ had not paid him. Drenched in desperation, my parents explained that the only possessions of value were their wedding rings and my mother's diamond earrings, an heirloom wedding gift from my maternal grandmother. The smuggler searched my parents and discovered that they had spoken the truth; they had nothing left to give. The smuggler stripped them of the wedding jewellery. These were precious items that were symbols of a prompt union, bringing my mother back to a day where she wore a borrowed dress and ate duck. A day so different to the unspeakable fear that now rested permanently on her face. She missed her sisters, her mother. Their constant fussing. The infinite sense of comfort that occurs when generations of women gather. She could see them at home looking out at the river and wondering about her, heavy with worry.

When the items were handed over to the smuggler, they were then taken to hide in a farmhouse set amid a field of palm trees.

The journey was taking its toll. Hồng Khanh had been bitten by various poisonous insects and had open sores on his legs. He was in agony, to the point where he could not walk properly. There was limited clean water. My mother gave Văn water from a pond. Already weak, he had now contracted severe dysentery.

Sispohon was the last checkpoint manned by Vietnamese forces. Soldiers regularly inspected each house in the area. That evening, my father was overcome with trepidation, dreading capture at any moment. As they listened to the soldiers making their inspections of various houses, fear exhaled from everyone's mouth and rumbled in silence through the house. Somehow, miraculously, they were not exposed.

The next morning, four men on bicycles took the group through the jungle. My father went first, then Hồng Khanh, then my mother with Văn, and finally Hải. A couple of the smugglers who spoke some Vietnamese explained that the wife and child of the man who was carrying my mother and Văn had been murdered by the Khmer Rouge. He spoke some French and was an educated man. They set off, the parties separated by a few kilometres to avoid suspicion. The men posed as merchants and my mother posed as the wife of the man whose bicycle she was sharing. None of the parties knew the fate of the others.

Before they reached their destination, the riders taking my father, Hải and Hồng Khanh demanded more money. When they found there was indeed none to be had, the smugglers abandoned each of the three men alone in the middle of the jungle near the border town of Poipet. In the fight between the Khmer Rouge and the Cambodian government, about six million landmines had been densely laid in and around the jungles of Poipet. My father and his nephew and brother-in-law were stranded in one of the world's largest minefields.

My father spotted a heavily trodden path made by merchants trading along the Cambodian–Thai border. But the jungle was dry and most of the large trees had been cut down. There weren't even vines from which he could rehydrate himself. The jungle was also sparse, which made it immensely difficult to hide. He saw scatterings of dead bodies and severed limbs. One decapitated head had been mounted on a wooden stake on which Vietnamese words had been written in blood: *Vietnamese are not welcome.* It was not clear to whom the words were directed. Perhaps it was a message from the Khmer Rouge to the Vietnamese forces who were trying to oust them. Whatever the case, it was a chilling and atrocious reminder of the danger that surrounded him. But there was only one way to go: forward.

My father decided to continue on the path, but not long after he was met by armed soldiers who did not wear any recognisable uniform. They wore khaki fatigues and had cartridge belts draped across them. They captured my father and took him to an enclosure surrounded by barbed wire. Here he met a Vietnamese helicopter pilot, also a refugee, as well as some Cambodians of Vietnamese descent. That night he was haunted by dreadful thoughts. There was no way any of the others could have made it, he reasoned. If they didn't die at the hand of soldiers, they would never survive the landmines or the lack of water. Occasionally, gunshots could be heard from the direction of the jungle. My father lay awake in terror.

The next morning, he discovered that the guerrillas who had captured him had contacted the Red Cross, who were operating near the border. For each refugee they safely delivered, the guerrillas were given a quantity of rice. In the morning, personnel from the Red Cross were brought to the enclosure and he was released to the Red Cross. They offered my father an aerogram with which to send a message to his family back home, but he refused it. The horrific journey he had endured and the thought of his missing son and wife had left him devoid of hope and the will to live. The devastation he felt was so pervasive, he could not face the empty and brutal reality that was before him. He had accumulated a heavy heart traumatised by re-education, landmines, guerrillas, severed limbs and gunshots. The trauma crept underneath his fingernails and into his eyes, his hair, his nostrils. My father promised himself that if he did not see my mother within a few days, he would take his own life.

·

Left alone in the jungle, Hồng Khanh had all but given up; his open sores had grown so infected he was rendered virtually immobile. Hải, who had been several kilometres behind when the smuggler had abandoned him, had decided to keep going in the hope of somehow catching up with Hồng Khanh. Hải had just caught sight of him—tall and fair, Hồng Khanh was easily recognisable especially in these surrounds as he was too fair to look Cambodian but could be mistaken for a Vietnamese soldier—when suddenly a patrol of Khmer Rouge soldiers emerged from the jungle. Shrinking into the shadows, Hải watched in horror as a blindfold was put around Hồng Khanh's head, signalling an execution was imminent. Then a large piece of wood was swung at Hồng Khanh's head. Instantly, his legs collapsed beneath him.

Awash with terror, Hải ran away as fast as he could. Then, in the distance, he saw my mother up ahead. The man who was transporting her had not abandoned her. Hải began to wave, calling out in Vietnamese to my mother. 'Aunty, stop! Stop!'

The man pedalled faster to get away from Hải. 'He's drawing too much attention,' he said to my mother. 'He's yelling in Vietnamese. If we stop we will all die!' My mother, unaware of what had happened to her youngest brother, understood what the man was saying and held on in frozen silence as they rode. The image of a screaming fifteen-year-old boy alone in a jungle, becoming smaller and smaller as they rode away, would haunt her forever.

The man gave my mother his sarong to wrap Văn in. It was a thin frayed cloth in stripes of black, green and brown with streaks of white. My brother Văn was fading. The man searched for the makeshift camp near the border where the Red Cross had established a small clinic in a tent. Instead of trading my mother for rice like the guerrillas did with my father, the man did not leave until he found a doctor. Somehow he contacted his uncle, who lived in the area. The uncle was fluent in French and there were French Red Cross personnel working in and around the area. With the uncle's help they found the clinic and the medical staff treated my brother. The uncle then asked a Red Cross officer whether my father was in the camp. My mother followed the two Cambodians and the Red Cross officer through the camp until they saw my father. Without a word, the man and his uncle left, leaving my mother reunited with my father, clasping the sarong tightly, speechless, hardly daring to believe she and her son were still alive; that amid the savagery of the jungles, soldiers and the smugglers, a lonely French-speaking Cambodian man had saved her.

To her relief, they were soon also reunited with Hải, but her pleasure in the reunion turned to mind-numbing grief as Hải described what had happened to Hồng Khanh.

When my mother received the news, her senses evaporated and formed a tomb above her. She suffered an aching, wrenching numbness as she imagined her stoic teenage brother blindfolded and surrounded by strange armed men in his last moments. *I should not have taken him*, she agonised. *It's my fault. I killed him. It is my fault he suffered such a brutal death.* At other times she persuaded herself that maybe Hải had been mistaken; that it wasn't her brother he had seen. Maybe he didn't get struck. Or maybe, though captured, instead of being killed he had been forced to become a child soldier. He was tall. Maybe he lived. The swirl of thoughts twisted around her and remained for a long time. Every so often throughout her life, these thoughts would revisit her and force her to once again taste the anguish, to smell the shame, to feel the sorrow, to hear guilt, to see the loss of her brother. She was the older sister; she had been responsible for him. Her own mother had pleaded with her to not take him but Hồng Khanh adored my mother and insisted on going where she went. My mother often said it was fate that it was Hải and not she who had witnessed what happened. Instead of fleeing as Hải did, she would have run to her brother and most likely been killed herself, along with Văn. She would have turned back.

As there were no official refugee camps in the area, the Red Cross moved my family to a Thai military camp. Here all the men, including my father, were ordered to dig trenches for the Thai soldiers engaged in border skirmishes with Cambodia. They were then moved to a prison that held Thai soldiers who had committed serious breaches of military codes. The prison was located on the Thai side of the Thai–Cambodia border in a district called Aranyaprathet. There were a few more Vietnamese people there but not many. At that camp, my father and Hải were made to clear the surrounding trees. The Thai prisoners were chained by their feet and they wore a metal ring around their necks. In the dark of the night, as the prisoners crawled and moved, the sounds of their rattling chains filled the air. The Thai guards who managed the prison regularly beat the Vietnamese as well as the prisoners, just for pleasure. Everyone was afraid the women would be raped, and the fear kept them all awake. My mother heard the grotesque, wild and violent sounds of random beatings and she tried hard to not be sick each time she heard human flesh being pounded. Some French-speaking

Vietnamese wrote on a small piece of paper about the fear of rape and beatings. Finally, when the Red Cross officers came to see them, these small notes were slipped into their hands.

Not long after, they were moved to an official refugee camp called Khao I Dang, twenty kilometres from Aranyaprathet. At the end of 1979, the United Nations had cleared the forest to make a camp for the Cambodians who were escaping the Khmer Rouge. It was administered by the Thai government and the United Nations. Ten out of the twelve sections of the camp were occupied by Cambodians; the remaining two housed Vietnamese.

The Cambodians in Khao I Dang were either hoping for resettlement to a third country or waiting for the situation to become safe for them to return home. There were rations of water, rice and canned fish. Though quantities were extremely limited, the rations were precious. So too was the relative peace; they could no longer hear the gunfire of the jungles or the screams of people being beaten. But although they had found refuge, the Vietnamese in the camp faced an uncertain future. At the time, no government had recognised as official refugees the Vietnamese who had left their country by foot; those in the camp were in limbo, with nowhere to go. My mother watched as people smashed their own heads against stone walls in desperation. It was the not knowing that became their new enemy. Some people's families offshore sent them money. Others were completely alone with no links to anyone. They could only hope that the faceless, nameless Powerful would soon decide that they were genuinely running from persecution. That they were running towards freedom.

The days ran into weeks as they waited for the world to recognise them as legitimate refugees. At the camp, there were interpreters who had worked for the Americans. They loved listening to the BBC and Voice of America on the radio. One day, there was an announcement by US president Jimmy Carter. As the English-speakers hovered around the radio, the other refugees were going about their routine activities, cooking, sleeping, praying. My mother remembers the sudden thunderous outbreak of joyful cries. The men ran around the camp shrieking the news. President Carter had officially recognised those Vietnamese who had travelled by foot to be refugees. The camp erupted in elation. The ecstatic roars of the crowd were deafening. People shook their heads in disbelief. Tears streamed and knees trembled with joy. People slumped to the ground with hands cupped in prayer.

Slowly, diplomats from all over the western world came to interview the refugees, including my family. Gough Whitlam, former prime minister of Australia, declared that he did not want anti-Communist Vietnamese refugees coming to Australia. Many would never forget his famous statement: 'I'm not having hundreds of fucking Vietnamese Balts coming into this country with their religious and political hatreds against us!' Fortunately, he was no longer prime minister at the time, and he no longer determined Australia's immigration policy.

My family was moved to Sikhiu refugee camp, situated in a mountainous region of Thailand. It was a former women's prison, converted into a camp to house the thousands of Vietnamese refugees flooding into the country, including numerous unaccompanied minors. All had travelled by foot through the sinister and dangerous jungles of Cambodia. The camp gathered people from all classes and ranks, with diverse stories and hopes. From criminals to CIA-trained intelligence officers, clergymen and scholars, one single fact bound them in solidarity: that no matter how, no matter why, they had survived. Within the four walls of this former prison, people ate, slept, studied, wrote, found love, gave birth and died. The cycle of life went on here just as it did in any other community in the world.

Though we were away from the mayhem of Cambodia and the oppression of Vietnam, Sikhiu refugee camp was not a complete haven. Every morning, all the refugees had to line up and salute the Thai flag while the Thai anthem played over the loudspeaker. Those who were too weak and hungry to attend were beaten. Sikhiu was notorious for the mistreatment of refugees. At night, the camp's Thai guards along with other local men broke into the camps and raped several women. The refugees were always on the alert.

In the camp everyone lived in makeshift shelters within a large compound. Each family sectioned off a little space with some wood and fabric. It was intensely crowded and at night there was literally no room to turn. Every day people would line up to get rations of water, rice, meat and oil so they could cook their own food among themselves. There was never enough food and water to go around.

Hải's mother had sewn pieces of gold into the hemline of his shirt and he was under strict instructions not to reveal the gold under any circumstances. Even when the smugglers abandoned him in the jungle, he held onto his gold. At the camp, it was Hải's gold that gave my parents enough capital to start a small enterprise. My mother cooked a variety of noodles and rice dishes and my father ground soya beans into soya milk. My mother, a natural entrepreneur with a warm smile, drew customers from all over the camp. They came with their money and with their stories. Women who were raped by guerrilla soldiers in the jungles of Cambodia spoke to her of their sense of shame. Young single men asked her to write faux love letters to potential suitors in America hoping to get money sent to them. Married men with families back in Vietnam came to her for advice because they had fallen in love with women at the camp. There were tabs with customers all over the camp who promised to pay. Some did, some didn't. With her exceptionally fair skin, European features and compassionate disposition, my mother was a source of support to many.

She did not realise that she was pregnant. Another refugee said that all pregnant women were permitted to have extra rations of food. My mother went to the central office to see whether she could get an extra ration for Văn. They did a pregnancy test and discovered that she was indeed pregnant.

One of the refugees at the camp was Lieutenant Colonel Cảnh, a former military doctor with the South Vietnamese Army. He asked the Thai guards whether he could use a small space in the guard's office at the camp to deliver me. The office was situated under a large tree on the western side of the camp. The birth was swift and the labour did not last long. The doctor was assisted by two Japanese volunteer nurses. It was there that I was born, two months premature after only two hours of labour: a tiny baby weighing two kilograms. Minutes after I drew my first breath, I was wrapped in the same sarong that the Cambodian man had given my mother. This simple stained cloth was woven with an unknown man's legacy of compassion, courage and integrity, a physical connection to a man's memories of his dead wife and child as he escorted my mother through the jungles. The Japanese nurses paraded me around the camp after I was born, chanting, 'Princess of Thailand, Princess of Thailand.' Later, when my father sent photographs to Vietnam from Australia, he would date and write a brief description on the back of each photo. Whenever I was in them, he would affectionately refer to me as 'Princess of Thailand'.

Occasionally there was entertainment at the camp. A lady by the name of Bùi Thị Tuyết Hồng, who was the wife of a senior Norwegian official, came from Norway and arranged for presents, concerts and sometimes an outdoor cinema. Hundreds of refugees would lie on the ground under the stars staring at the screen. For a brief hour, as voices of enlarged characters stretched against a dark sky, bellowed across the hills surrounding Sikhiu, they felt the dignity of being human.

Many French and Thai Christian priests came to visit the camps and they gave the refugees money. The generosity and immense compassion they exhibited was disarming. Neither my mother's family nor my father's had any Christian tradition, but it was these Christian priests who helped my mother to pray, to ease the pain of being alive while her brother lay murdered somewhere in the Poipet jungle. They coaxed her senses back to life. It was the gentleness and concern of these quiet Christians that rescued her sanity. She didn't know who Mary was, or what Jesus looked like, but she was thankful that these strangers prayed for her. She appreciated the fact that they listened.

As diplomats from all over the world visited the camp to help resettle the refugees in third countries, my parents met with Australian representatives. The Canadians processed refugees the fastest—people could generally leave within a month—but rumour spread throughout the camp that it was a chokingly cold place, which didn't appeal to those who were used to the humidity of South Vietnam. The US was out of the question, as my father still resented the Americans for leaving South Vietnam undefended. Australia had the advantage of being relatively close to Vietnam, and my father's brother had already arrived there, having travelled by boat. It was decided: we would go to Australia.

An Australian government representative who interviewed my father had left behind a magazine about Australian lifestyle, encouraging the refugees to look through it. My father savoured the coloured pictures. He turned to a page that had a large bearded man sitting at a country pub with a beer. The man wore a sleeveless shirt and was covered in tattoos. This was my father's first visual representation of Australia. He was terrified! One of the Christian volunteers gave us the address of a Vietnamese Catholic priest living in Adelaide. We could write to him and he would help connect us to the Catholic community in Australia.

My family moved to a transit camp near Bangkok in readiness for our departure to Australia. There were rats the size of cats which bit many unsuspecting arrivals, but we were immensely glad to be there. We stayed at that camp for one month, during which there were no rations for water. The distribution of food and supplies was disorderly. Văn, having spent half of his young life at the previous camp, surrounded by men and women who cherished him, cried to return. At close to two years old, 'Sikhiu' was one of the first words he connected to an extended family of circumstancial uncles and aunts who had given him snacks and taught him how to sing Vietnamese children's songs. But while Văn howled 'Sikhiu, Sikhiu', my parents savoured their reprieve, knowing we were one step further away from the carnage they still so vividly remembered.

On the day we were to leave, I came down with diarrhoea. My mother didn't dare take me to the clinic or tell anyone, for fear we wouldn't be allowed on the plane. She wiped me clean as best she could and wrapped me tightly in the old sarong. Even though I was heavy with excrement I didn't cry. Together with four other Vietnamese refugee families, we boarded the Qantas plane. There were no other Asians aboard.

This was my family's first plane ride and it was a one-way trip to an unknown land. We took off, and my parents watched as the land beneath us shrank smaller and smaller like a fading winter shadow. We flew high above lost stories in the Killing Fields, the barbed wire and landmines, and away from Hồng Khanh. Sitting on the plane heading towards Australia, my parents didn't yet feel relief. They didn't allow themselves to become complacent about the risks of returning to the horrors of Cambodia and Vietnam. They had faced and survived peril after peril. Nothing was certain, even now. So they all sat in apprehensive silence as the white people around them chatted politely. They were frightened that at any moment the shred of possibility they were so delicately sitting on would be disturbed. It seemed that even as a baby, Văn understood this. He was quiet and still throughout the journey.

When the flight attendants served us food, my parents panicked, fearing we had to pay for it. They had nothing except the clothes they were wearing and the sarong in which I was wrapped. With the meal was served a can of Coca-Cola. When the Americans had come to Vietnam, as well as bringing military support for the South they had brought this strangely delicious luxury drink. Many South Vietnamese consumed it only during the sacred Lunar New Year festival of Tết. After the war ended in 1975, my mother hadn't seen a can of Coca-Cola again. Now, five years later, on a Qantas plane, an Australian flight attendant gave her a can. She stared at it. It was in this moment that she finally believed that the terror and the crippling waiting were truly over. The red and white can which she had not seen since the fall of Saigon meant freedom. The new life that beckoned them manifested itself in an aluminium can. It meant they were away from the contamination of prison camps, brutal rapes, guerrillas and constant, devouring fear.

It was only from this moment that my mother was finally filled with relief. It was as though she had been holding her breath for years. Clutching the Coca-Cola and her three-month-old baby, my mother wept, almost in disbelief. We were alive.

CHAPTER 3

Jesus will help us

Even though it was the end of a typical Australian spring, my parents felt a fierce and chilly wind. It was 13 November 1980. We had arrived in Australia as one of the first few refugee families who had travelled by foot across Cambodia into Thailand. My mother remembers later being interviewed on radio, prodded with questions about the remarkable journey.

Our first port of entry into Australia was Perth airport. The air was crisp; the blanket of humidity common to South-East Asia had been left behind. My parents froze in their inadequate clothes. In the transit lounge, there were a couple of Australian women in overcoats waiting for their connecting flight. They looked at us. Our skin was tanned, our clothes worn. We were mute, frightened aliens. My father would never forget the compassion and pity he saw in their eyes. He had seen other eyes from jungles and prisons—violent, angry and lustful—and though the women did not speak, he knew in his heart their eyes were welcoming and that his family was safe in Australia. Together with the other four Vietnamese families, we were then transferred to Sydney.

Upon arriving in Sydney, we were met by two representatives from the Department of Immigration and then transported by a small bus to the Villawood Migrant Hostel. Years later this facility would become notorious as the Villawood Immigration Detention Centre, surrounded by tall barbed-wire fencing to contain asylum seekers as if they were vicious animals. On the bus ride to the hostel, my mother gazed in absolute awe at the clean, wide streets and the large beautiful houses. The spring blooms had started to open and displayed their stunning petals to her like a thousand glistening ballerinas. She was intoxicated and realised just how far from Vietnam they were.

Within the hostel compound were refugees from all over the world—Vietnam, Cambodia and Iran. Like us, they had journeyed thousands of kilometres from the ancient lands of their ancestors to finally converge in this suburban facility. Some of their children had sad and worn eyes, others played naively. The adults were supportive of each other through broken bits of English. My father recalls a pleasant and hopeful atmosphere. Most of us had already been processed as refugees offshore. There was no barbed wire, and people moved about freely inside and outside the facility. Christian volunteers visited regularly, providing the residents with clothes and other essentials. My parents were overwhelmed by the warmth and generosity of the nuns and volunteers from the Catholic charity St Vincent de Paul. My mother and I would later become devoted fans of their second-hand stores. No matter where we were in Sydney, we could always count on a nearby St Vinnies, as they became affectionately known, for daywear, furniture, kitchenware and party costumes.

On our first night at Villawood, we were allocated sleeping quarters. My mother, Văn and I were in one room and my father and Hải in another. We didn't know if we would be given meals or when dinner time was, so we sat quietly in our rooms, creatures that had been buffeted and weathered into submission—afraid that any questions or movements would upset the fragile tranquillity we had found. Dinner time came and went. Familiar hunger pangs bellowed. Finally, other Vietnamese refugees who had arrived earlier realised we weren't at dinner and came to our rooms to see what was wrong. They saw us waiting placidly. On realising what had happened, they went back to their own rooms and brought us instant noodles. As we ate, my mother, full of uncertainty in this new land and already anxious about how to support her family, asked them whether they knew how Vietnamese people could make money.

'What will we do here? How do we make a living?'

'Don't worry, there's plenty of work. You can sew, work in a factory, clean. That's what I hear from the settled ones. It will be alright.'

•

Summer arrived with an unfamiliar blistering dry heat. We were going through the process of creating a new life. The first step was to be disease free and so we were taken to a hospital to get vaccinations. The next thing was banking, even though we had no money. Representatives of the major banks came to Villawood to encourage the refugees to open bank accounts. The Commonwealth Bank of Australia was the first to market to us so that's who earned our loyalty. (Years later when Văn and I needed to open bank accounts, naturally the Commonwealth Bank of Australia was our first choice.) We were free to stay at the migrant hostel until we found housing and were ready to go. During the day the refugees left when they needed to and came back in the evenings. There was no pressure to leave.

My uncle, Thanh, who is my father's brother, and his wife had arrived in Australia earlier, having left by boat. They were all reunited when Uncle Thanh and his wife came to visit us at the hostel. It was a surreal moment when the brothers saw each other for the first time in years, knowing that they had both cheated death and were now meeting on foreign soil in a land without gunfire or random incarceration. The last time they had seen each other was at home—a whole dimension away in time and place. They spoke of their sisters in Vietnam, their countless nieces and nephews working in the rice fields. They thought of their mother, dressed in her southern Vietnamese peasant pyjamas, so far from her only sons.

Ever since my father had seen the image of the tattooed Australian man in a pub in the magazine in Thailand, it had haunted him. One of the first things he asked Uncle Thanh was: 'Are Australian men scary? Are they violent and mean?'

My uncle laughed heartily. 'No, that's just on the outside. They're very kind.'

It was true that my parents' first impressions of Australians were that they were immensely hospitable and compassionate. Australia had truly welcomed them. Their only complaint was the food. Dinner at the hostel was the typical Anglo meat-and-three-veg combo. Although they were extremely grateful to be fed, they missed the taste of home—of lemongrass, garlic, chilli, fish sauce and mint. After the immediate nightmares and trauma started to melt away, the culinary desire for home came back.

One night, asleep in our room at the hostel, my mother sensed a strange presence. When she awoke, she saw a dark-haired white man standing at the foot of the bed. He was completely naked. She grabbed Văn and me tightly and screamed. The man ran outside. After this incident and riddled with familiar fear, she insisted to my father that it was time to leave the hostel and venture out to find a home of our own, away from the full-time support of helpful Australian hostel staff. Hải went to live with my aunt and uncle who had settled earlier. Like the other four families who came from Thailand with us on 13 November 1980, we each dispersed from the migrant hostel and settled across Sydney to dream another narrative—leaving behind Sikhiu, giant rats and regular Anglo meals.

The first place we moved to was a room below a staircase in Alexandria Street, Newtown—an inner-city suburb four kilometres southwest of Sydney's central business district. The lodging was a basement of some sort. It was cheap, dark and damp. We had one uncovered mattress to sleep on and, courtesy of St Vinnies, a black and white television. Many years later, I would drive my family back to Newtown, where my parents pointed out the old terrace house in which we'd lived. When my parents told me of the staircase, I remembered a children's pop-up book where a lion or some other wild creature lived underneath the stairs unbeknownst to the family. In the book the space below the staircase was a magic entranceway to another world of wonderful fantasies and new pleasures. I wondered what the occupants above the stairs must have thought of us: a dishevelled non-English-speaking Vietnamese couple with a four-month-old baby and a two-year-old son. They were wild things from another realm. By-products of a war that many young Australians visibly protested against. Here they were below the stairs. *What to do. What to do.*

My mother was still in deep despair from the lingering tragedy of losing Hồng Khanh. It was six months before she could eat properly. Anxiety and sorrow buried themselves in her stomach and she suffered constant cramps and pains. Somehow, the doctors who treated her concluded the problem was with her teeth, so they decided to take them out. At twenty-seven years old she had a full set of dentures. Without a word of English to object and without the energy to protest, my mother let it all happen. But the dentures did not help to bring her back from the dark pit of despair. Recalling the comfort she had derived from the prayers of the Christians at the Sikhiu camp, she decided that was what we needed.

My parents wrote to the Catholic priest in Adelaide whose address we had been given at Sikhiu. He put us in touch with Father Dominic Nguyễn Văn Đời, also a refugee and one of the very first Vietnamese Catholic priests in Australia at the time. We did six months of lessons at a local church. With very little English my parents tried hard to comprehend Jesus and how to be good Catholics in this new land. The priest in Adelaide contacted some lovely Australians to be our godparents. Once Father Dominic was settled, he travelled the country to baptise Vietnamese people and to hold mass in Vietnamese.

The hour of mass was a sacred and treasured timeslot that allowed fragmented and ruptured souls to come together as a community. Once a month clusters of Vietnamese clung to each other over prayers in Catholic churches around Sydney, relishing the sound of the Vietnamese language being spoken and celebrated. We would pray for salvation, for our brethren back home, for extra shifts, for better days. When we were ready, Father Dominic came and baptised us in the sight of our godparents. I was christened Catherine. My mother was Mary, my father Paul and Văn became Peter. Later, after my younger brother was born, he was christened John Bosco. So began my parents' spiritual journey towards some sliver of healing.

•

Eventually we left the little space in Newtown because it was ridden with fleas and other microscopic parasites. My small body was covered in bites. Marrickville, three kilometres southwest of Newtown, was our next destination. The suburb was home to the calloused knuckles and weathered foreheads of migrants from Greece, Vietnam and many places in between.

My earliest recollections are of our life in Marrickville. We moved into an old brick split-level terrace house on Illawarra Road. The house had a huge driveway which inclined upward like a concrete sea serpent. It rose gradually until it formed a horizon with the government housing commission flats that always seemed to me to be suspended from somewhere in the sky behind us. One of my first memories is of playing hide and seek with Văn and some neighbourhood children, looking up towards the flats and then skywards, distracted by the fast movement of the bloated clouds. The sky was darkening and a wind had blown up. Leaves were dancing around the yard. I remember being lost in those moments just before the impending storm, in the curious quiet on the verge of mayhem.

Our terrace was opposite the Marrickville branch of the Returned and Services League (RSL club). The RSL is an organisation set up to support men and women who served or are serving in the Australian Defence Force. Licensed clubs were created as a place where war veterans could meet. They serve subsidised drinks and food and a lot of revenue comes from the poker machines installed inside the clubs.

I remember the giant Australian flag and the large bronze statues of Australian soldiers by the front wall at the club's entrance. The statues were frozen in time, saluting. They wore the slouch hat, iconic of Australian soldiers. The Southern Cross constellation was in the background. Many people who came home to Marrickville on the train passed by the statues. I wondered what those soldiers would have made of the stream of people alighting at the station, a diverse mix that over the years would come from Africa, the Middle East, the Mediterranean and Asia. The soldiers' watchful, reserved gaze would also see the streets change. Buildings would be torn down and developed into offices and community centres. Ultimately the RSL itself, together with the gallant bronze soldiers, would be demolished, giving way to high-rise modern apartments.

Our neighbours in Marrickville were also refugees from Vietnam, although they had left by boat like many others. They were three little boys and their mother and father, along with a teenage aunt. They kindly inducted us into life in Australia. My mother did not have any technical skills. Our neighbour taught her how to sew and piece bits of pre-cut fabric together. Once my adaptable mother had learned to recognise the staple pieces that formed pants, shirts and dresses, our neighbours helped her to find work sewing in a factory.

I remember her leaving to go to work for the first time. I was left in the care of our neighbour, the young aunt. My mother snuck out of the house via the side entrance. It was a long and narrow path that was unevenly paved with tosses of stone. The world away from my mother's proximity, the safety of her smell, was terrifying—the cars, the beetles, the wet tissues and plastic bags that gathered in the gutter after the rain, the roar of the trains erupting over the railway bridge. I don't know how I knew she was leaving, but I sensed that raw moment of initial separation from my mother. The disappearance of the film of her proximity was palpable, like the sudden departure of a spring sun shower, or that brief second when you know you've lost the battle with the wind and the kite string slips from your grip.

I evaded the babysitter's feeble attempts at distraction and escaped her grasp, running down the long side entrance to glimpse my mother's silhouette exiting the left side of the house. Screaming with a lungful of desperation, I ran down the sidewalk. Everything seemed too big. Beyond the door was a blinding white confusing mash of world. All I saw was my mother at the cusp of it all, about to melt into the vortex. Behind me a voice yelled, 'Cat Thao! Come back! Let Mum go to work! She has to go to work!' I didn't know what this Work was. Nor did I care.

My mother snuck off successfully that time, but she wasn't always able to leave without tiny arms and fingers having to be prised from around her neck through storms of weeping.

As it turned out, though, my mother wouldn't work outside the home for very long. Common with most Vietnamese refugee mothers, she would spend the next twenty years as an outworker operating a sweatshop in one of our rooms. The Singer sewing machine and Juki industrial overlocker would become as familiar to us as family members. Wherever we moved, they came with us, like precious heirlooms. They watched over us like the ghosts of ever-present ancestors. There is a photo taken on my fourth birthday. Văn and I are wearing animal party hats. His was a smiling crocodile; mine was a yellow giraffe with a brown tuft of hair. Văn isn't smiling. My mother is also in the photo, dressed in her St Vinnies clothes. Arranged in front of us on the coffee table are a bottle of Fanta, a packet of chocolate éclairs and a birthday cake. I have a bandage on the inside of my right elbow covering an outbreak of the terrible eczema I suffered from growing up. Standing impassively in the background of the photo is the Juki overlocker: sombre, firm, disciplined, reliable. Like a grandfather clock.

Two years later when I turned six, Văn and I resumed our positions, this time in front of the Singer sewing machine. Văn has a faint smile this time. I stand erect and attentive, albeit with a cheeky grimace. We are again wearing animal party hats. Remarkably, I still have the giraffe, while Văn has changed to a frog. He's much taller than in the previous photo whereas I seem not to have changed much. Knowing my mother, she probably kept all the hats and candles from the previous birthday, along with the fake white and yellow daisies and chrysanthemums in a vase on the coffee table. There is another birthday cake, probably from the same bakery in Marrickville. An owl-shaped children's blackboard is leaning against the Fanta bottle. A stack of plastic cups sits beside it. Large rolls of black thread have been inserted in the rods of the Singer. There are piles of pre-cut fabric on the table beside the machine. Even now, I can tell from the photo that it is a combination of satin and chiffon—delicate and hard to sew.

Often I would come home from school, whether it was second grade or seventh, and help my mother unstitch hundreds of incorrectly sewn garments. When some designer from an upmarket Surry Hills studio decided to be adventurous with their line, producing highly complex designs, my mother would spend hours unstitching the sample and slowly piecing it back together. It would result in something that would be draped over a half-starved model paid several hundred times what my mother would earn for an hour's work and, accordingly to the life insurers, the model's life was worth so much more than ours.

Sitting atop a large pile of fabric, I would listen with my mother to the Vietnamese program on the Special Broadcasting Service (SBS) radio station, specifically established to serve the needs of ethnic communities. She would work late into the night. On many occasions when I couldn't sleep or I awoke suddenly, I would find her underneath the orange spotlight, asleep at the machine, its constant hum buzzing in her ear like a lovely monsoon mosquito. I would always try to press the off button quietly so as not to wake her. I held my breath and put gentle pressure on the button. But the action, no matter how careful I was, would always jerk her awake.

'Mum, go to sleep.'

'What are you doing up? Go to sleep. I have to finish this. There's a deadline.'

I remember the times when one of the machines would break. My mother, ever graceful, calm and never in a moment of panic, would get her kit of tiny Phillips-head screwdrivers and screws and try to fix it. As a six-year-old, I learned how to change broken needles and worn out bits of the machine. I could thread the Singer skilfully and change its oil. Opening up the machine to reveal the small sunken pool of machine oil was a fascinating expedition. It was like an unmasking of a mysterious story character. My wild imagination would lead me to stand beside the machine in a hypnotic trance. I would daydream, watching the droplets of oil build up in weight, then descend with a plop into the pool below. I imagined an allied machine wounded in the battle to rescue my family from local government inspectors or vicious landlords. Or picture microscopic ballerina fairies, which everyone else would only see as specks of dust through the Venetian blinds, slicing and swimming through the humid air above the pool of oil.

I would always fall asleep to the regular sound of my mother sewing—the coded sounds of the rapid fire of the needle as she stepped on the pedal, then the quick click of the end of a consecutive series of stitches as she snapped her heel. Sometimes her eyes were so tired and the scent of sleep so seductive, she would place her fingers too far in and the needle would stab into the nail of her forefinger. Through gritted teeth, she would tend quickly to the wound with Eagle Brand green medicated oil and keep going. The tune of the sewing machines, like the regularity of rust and rain, became the lullaby of my childhood. Delivery-day deadlines became the milestones upon which each week was measured.

•

Shortly after we moved to Marrickville, my father went to the Commonwealth Employment Service office to look for work. Manual labour didn't require much English so he was able to get a job swiftly. He worked as a sander at a carpentry factory in Sydenham, only one train station away. But to save money my father walked to work and back each day. At the factory he met another Vietnamese man who was leaving for a better-paying job at Lidcombe, several kilometres west, with a company called Sigma Industries. It manufactured air-conditioning systems for trains. The man got my father a job at this factory, and he began to take the train to work. My father was overjoyed as the pay was great. At the time my mother was making $162 a week at the sewing factory. They were able to buy a second-hand Mazda for $300. It was the first asset they could call their own, earned through toiling with their hands and feet, an acquisition which gave them a whisper of pride. They didn't dare aspire to own any other luxuries; in those days, an apple, a uniform, an automatic car and a living family were enough.

But after six months, work at the air-conditioning factory dried up and my father was unemployed. Soon after, he got a job at Crown Corning's glassware factory in Waterloo, a few kilometres south of Sydney's CBD. It was shift work. Every three days the shifts would change, moving between afternoon, day and night shifts. My mother was still working at the factory and there was no one to look after my brother and me. My father looked for another job and found work as a kitchen-hand and dishwasher at Eastern Suburbs Leagues Club near Bondi Junction, not far from the famed and stunning Bondi Beach. It gave him a glimpse into a different class, a world where men wore collared shirts and sliced their knives through juicy steaks. My father was off Tuesdays and Thursdays and could work out a schedule with my mother to look after us. The hours were good but there wasn't any parking for non-members of the club so my father had to park about a twenty-five-minute walk away. He left to work as a machine operator for F. Muller, a company which manufactured refrigeration units. He stayed there for over fifteen years.

During the time my mother worked at the sewing factory, the ritual of hide and seek continued while I cried and pleaded each morning. One day, seeing how much her Princess of Thailand needed her, my mother stayed home. For good. My father rotated through day, afternoon and night shifts at the factory while my mother sewed at home. They mastered the routine and rhythm of a new life, hoping it would be as predictable and steady as possible.

•

One of my mother's older brothers, Uncle Căng, was finally released from the re-education camp and he too left Vietnam.

Uncle Căng migrated to Australia via the Sikhiu refugee camp and came to live with us. He was dark and unshaven, with an unruly moustache. My first memory of him was when he and my mother were walking towards the intersection of Marrickville and Illawarra roads, my mother carrying me. He stretched out his arms to hold me, but I turned away violently and gripped my mother, fearful of this scary-looking person.

I would later discover that this strange dark man was a broken-hearted poet and an imprisoned former police officer of the South Vietnamese government. For the next eight or so years before his wife and three daughters were sponsored to come over to Australia, with each payday from his factory job he would buy fish and chips for Văn and me. Thursday afternoon would come around and I would sit on his knee as we tore open the deep-fried packets of salty goodness wrapped in a single sheet of paper. It was always an eagerly awaited divine ritual of delight.

As a man with charisma and clear leadership capacity, my uncle would ascend from being a simple factory worker to production manager of an entire factory plant which produced a variety of industrial netting. In his lunch breaks, he would compose traditional Vietnamese poetry. Sometimes, within the confines of his backyard, among the polystyrene boxes in which he grew mint and shallots, he would sorrowfully recite these compositions. His tone was always mournful, his songs always yearning for yesterday. They were always performed on drunken occasions accompanied by nostalgic cigarette smoke rings which appeared and faded abruptly like a look of knowing in a lover's eyes.

Later, when I was old enough to appreciate the irony and tragedy of his life, he would give to me what he described as his life's treasures—the collection of handwritten poems of an unremarkable Australian life, composed over decades on the loud factory floor. That day, tears welling in my eyes as I cradled in my hands his memories, his songs, a man's lifetime of love and loss, I felt unworthy of the privilege—to be the keeper of this compilation of bitter hopes, solitary moments and hushed, brave dreams.

Before Uncle Căng's wife and daughters arrived, he and father would meet regularly with the few other men from Tây Ninh province now living in Sydney. Each week, the blue plastic sheet taken from the excess stock at my uncle's factory was laid down on the concrete in our backyard, the housing commission flats still supervising the curious activity below. My mother would make food that went well with lingering laughter and iced beer. Back in Vietnam most people didn't have fridges, so beer was drunk with ice to keep it cool. Here in Australia, even with fridges, somehow the subconscious ritual of plonking cubes of ice into beer beamed them back to the familiar land of their ancestors. I would always watch on with a sense of hesitation and splendour.

One Christmas, my uncle built a manger out of crumpled paper, sprayed with silver paint to look like stone. He took coloured netting from the factory and decorated the manger with Christmas baubles and other found objects. Then he added porcelain statues of Baby Jesus, Joseph, Mary and smiling sheep, purchased from—of course—St Vinnies. Looking back, the haphazard attempt to recreate the nativity scene must have been hideous bordering on blasphemous.

Uncle Căng and my father unfolded the blue plastic sheet and the rhythm of the evening began to set in. The men sat and started to gulp the Fosters with a Vietnamese count of 'One, two, three—down!' Glasses clinked as the past crept in to join them.

My cousin Hải had come to stay with us during his summer holiday from school. My mother had prepared and hid presents for Văn and me inside the house. Close to midnight Hải and my mother ran outside and said to me, 'Santa is here! He's inside!' I stood with Văn at the door, petrified. I did not want to see a fat white man in a red outfit that didn't have matching red shoes, even though I was fairly sure he wouldn't eat me. Finally, after what seemed like a very long period of hovering on the threshold, paralysed by fear, Văn ran into the house and then out. But Santa was too fast for Văn. Hải pointed to the sky and said, 'There he goes! Look!' I strained with all my strength to see him fly off but I must have been too slow. Was it because my parents couldn't speak English and he wasn't sure whether we could speak English either? Later I would wonder why Jesus, Santa and the fairy godmother, as well as the cast of *Home and Away*, were all white.

When my first tooth began to wobble I became excited at the prospect of being visited by the tooth fairy. I wondered whether

her fluttering would sound like a mosquito near my ear. The evening after I had pulled out the tooth, I placed it under my pillow hoping for at least one dollar. With that, I could buy three bags of liquorice at the school tuckshop. I examined the tooth carefully, making sure all the blood was cleaned off the crown and the root. In the morning, I looked underneath the pillow. The tooth was still there. Maybe the tooth fairy had forgotten. Or maybe she hadn't come because I wasn't white. On television, the kids that were visited by the tooth fairy were white with white parents. I kept my tooth in a little box in the top drawer of my desk. Just in case.

The night was coloured a blackish blue. As I pondered how fast Santa had disappeared, I noticed my father and his friends growing more and more inebriated. My mother and I would soon come to recognise this pattern which became a motif in our lives. First there were the loud voices, followed by roaring belly laughs, and finally some sort of song. The songs all centred on the old days, on their beloved Vietnam. Afterwards, when the Past had flirted with the men and danced her way out with the smells of the night, my mother would pack away the glasses and clear the dishes. Some of the men stumbled home, others sprawled on the floor of the living room of our rented house. If my father was still conscious, my mother would attempt to scold him for drinking too much. But in his state of bliss, there was no more gunfire, no more camps, no more dirty factory earplugs, no more day and night shifts. All that was left was the peaceful hymn of a temperamental river in Gò Dầu, far, far away.

It was 1984. We had been in Australia for four years but we still didn't have enough money for a telephone because the monthly landline fees were very high. Every single surplus dollar was sent back to nourish our relatives in Vietnam. Aching with the need to hear the voices from a distant homeland, my mother went to the post office to send a telex to the family in Vietnam to arrange a date for a phone call. Ten family members in Vietnam travelled for an hour and a half from Gò Dầu to the ornate French-built post office in Ho Chi Minh City, the only place within a day's travel that had telephones permitted for international connection. Hundreds of people came from provinces all over South Vietnam to wait for their One Phone Call. They sprawled on the ground, floating in and out of sleep, eating the small packets of food they had brought, too scared to move in case they were called. Hours went by. In Sydney, we gathered at the home of a friend who owned a telephone. We dialled. In Ho Chi Minh City, the family was called. We were connected. The muffled voices and sobs of relief, nostalgia and joy seeped through the crackling line. Through tears, my mother yelled, 'Stop crying! We're wasting the minutes!' But no one was able to adhere to this instruction. Even if it were merely cries, for a few brief minutes, my mother could hear the cherished voice of her own mother through the telephone's umbilical-like cord. She could imagine the humidity, the shards of green rice and the malnourished frames of her brothers and sisters. It had been five years since she had heard the voices of her siblings and the slur of her mother's speech from years of chewing betel nuts.

My father trembled as he spoke to his mother. They were both more softly spoken than the relatives on my mother's side.

That first telephone call knocked at the deep yearning for home that my parents buried daily. It was as if they had awoken from a restless slumber in this new Australian life. And when the receiver was replaced in its cradle, the silence ravaged them.

•

My parents continued to work hard and their thrifty lifestyle enabled them to accumulate some money. They found a small business for sale: a shop selling newspapers and magazines. My mother's entrepreneurial flair had resurfaced, and the loans and papers had all been processed; all they needed to do was sign. But on reflection, my mother told my father that she couldn't do it. Her children needed her, and if they bought the shop, it would absorb all her time and her attention on us would drift. No. We had to stay close together for as long as possible. This new home was a big world of Australian uncertainty and she wanted to be there for us, for as long as she could.

But to my distress, it wasn't possible to remain always and forever in my mother's company. Reluctantly, I started preschool with fears of all-encompassing abandonment. I was to be left in the care of smiling Australian ladies with blue eye shadow and permed hair and I was terrified. I didn't speak any English and I couldn't even tell them I wanted to go to the toilet. But my squeaky sandals made me braver. They made a noise with every step I took so my mother would be able to hear me. Văn, who was always strong and fearless, left preschool for St Brigid's primary school. We were both to be in Catholic schools for most of our primary and high school education. With our baptisms came my parents' relentless determination to school their children at expensive Catholic schools. Like their parents before them, our parents were firm believers in the value of education. They were determined that we would go to good schools, no matter what the cost. Jesus would help us.

CHAPTER 4

An Australian dream, a Vietnamese garden

After several years of sewing garments, day and night factory shifts, and Vietnamese prayer, my parents had saved enough for a deposit on a house. My mother had a cousin who was living in Punchbowl, a suburb ten kilometres southwest of Marrickville. The cousin had left Vietnam by boat and arrived in Australia a few years earlier. Eager to be close to family, my parents bought a house in Punchbowl on Beauchamp Street. We pronounced it Bee-chum and none of us ever figured out where the punch bowl of Punchbowl really was. I loved our five years there. The house represented our piece of the Australian dream. There is a photo of us all standing out the front: my mother and father, Hải and my uncle, the poet, Văn and I. We are all proudly perched against the café latte–coloured Datsun 120Y my parents had bought when we moved to Punchbowl. The car is parked behind my uncle's 1979 mustard-coloured Corona. My mother is wearing a second-hand jumper with a picture of Halley's Comet on it and my father has a Clark Gable moustache. I am in pink patent leather shoes far too large for me. I remember begging my uncle to buy me those pre-loved shoes at the Flemington flea market one Saturday morning. In the photo, the sun is shining. My father has his hands on his hips and is standing tall, holding in his pockets Stitched-Together-Patches-of-Possibility. Dreaming just enough.

The house was on a quiet leafy street. It had whitewashed walls and our number was painted white inside a black oval on the right-hand side of the entrance. My father planted hydrangeas, bougainvillea, poinsettias and daisies in the front garden, which had a concrete path that curved into the patio. On the left was a side entrance leading to the backyard, which was enclosed by a tall white picket fence. The yard at the back was an enormous wonderland. My father decided to grow his little patch of Vietnam all the way at the end of the yard in the right-hand corner. There were clumps of lemongrass, mint, shallots, purple perilla leaves and coriander, as well as orange, lemon, peach and banana trees, and vegetables on vines that climbed, sprawled and twisted into themselves. It was an enchanting plot that he was proud of. The vines and tendrils created a substantial canopy over the few square metres. I would pass through an imaginary wall and find myself on the other side, emerging underneath a cool shelter of lush leaves with webbed rays of sunlight filtering through. I would stand on the naked earth, perfectly raked, ready for me to ruin. There is a photo of Văn standing in the garden. He must have been about eight. He is wearing brown corduroys, a white striped shirt and a broad smile. His right arm is outstretched and poised, his hand cradling a cluster of fruit—the first of the season.

We had seven cats. They kept breeding. We had no idea about desexing. Occasionally as the darkness descended on a thick summer evening, my mother, father, Văn and I would pack the Datsun. I would be clutching a few of the scrawny kittens, pacifying them in the backseat with tender strokes. Every now and then my father would hear a yelp from me as the kittens clawed into my hand. We would cruise through the unlit streets of Punchbowl like stealth hunters. Sometimes we would lurk in the surrounding suburbs. When my father spotted a backyard he deemed dark enough he would slow down the car. But I always argued against the first choice, declaring it was not a good enough home. When we finally settled on a place, I would hold my breath, my heart smacking against my chest, as we dropped the meowing kittens over the fence. But no matter how long it took, sometimes many months, they would always find their way back home.

The childless couple next door adored me. The wife would watch me play. She told me she had had seven miscarriages, though at the time I didn't understand what a miscarriage was. She tried to explain it to me over the fence one day. I couldn't understand how a baby got inside a tummy in the first place, and then how it could disappear. Did it explode into a thousand bits of glitter? I shrugged and went back to playing Monkey Magic with Văn. *Monkey Magic* was a TV series on the ABC based on the sixteenth-century Chinese novel *Journey to the West* and featured a monk, a pig monster obsessed with lust and gluttony, a water monster who was a reforming cannibal and a magic monkey. Together they went on a pilgrimage to fetch the Holy Scriptures, battling demons and monsters along the way. The Japanese-produced show had been dubbed into English by the BBC. Văn and I were fascinated with the stream of crazy characters and jumped around the backyard with broomsticks, doing karate chops and spins. Văn and I were always going on adventures. We would sneak down the back laneway and slip through a gap in a neighbour's fence to steal berries from a tree.

As we settled into our own glimpse of Australian dream, my parents still carried their old home with them in their mouths—from conversation to cuisine. Inside the house, we spoke, ate and lived Vietnamese. Sometimes when I got home from school I would be greeted by two little black and orange moths on the doorstep, both comfortably perched on the incline facing one another. I would step over them and head to the kitchen, which would be filled with the aroma of fried salted lemongrass fish. I would hover around my mother like a kitchen god's silent prayer. I would tell my mother over the sizzle of fish that the ancestors had come to pay us a visit and she would remind me never to step on them. To this day, I've never crushed a moth—just in case.

•

Vietnamese people started arriving in greater numbers, some from Tây Ninh province. My parents started a money-lending syndicate. In developing countries, where collateral for bank loans is usually scarce, families or groups of close friends rely on informal money-lending syndicates. Funds are pooled together and loans are given out each month. A $500 syndicate of twenty people would yield a potential monthly loan pool of $10,000 with differing interest rates each month. The interest rates were a way to fairly determine who each month's borrower would be. It was simple: everybody would secretly write down the interest they were willing to pay on the loan if they were granted it at that month's meeting. Everyone's piece of paper would be folded up and then placed on the dining table in a clear vertical line. My mother would then unfold each one in front of the participants. The person willing to pay the highest interest, and therefore the most desperate person for the loan, would be granted it that month. As the organisers of the syndicate, my parents could access the pool of loan funds interest-free. There were no contracts, no way to enforce repayments of the loans; there was only one sacred rule: trust.

Each month, my parents would host the syndicate meeting which consisted only of close family and friends. We Vietnamese had to stick together and leverage our network. Each month the women would cook a variety of food. Some couples went to farms far out in Western Sydney to buy fresh ducks to make congealed duck blood salad. It was always a special occasion when a live duck was bought. Everyone participated in a stage of preparation, whether it was roasting peanuts, grinding peppercorns, slicing the mint, making the fish sauce or holding the bowl of blood. There was a communal festive air in the momentum of production, like we were celebrating in some village in the countryside of Vietnam—but instead of mud huts and rice fields there were tiled floors and local council regulations to adhere to.

The duck, its feet and beak tied together, would flap wildly as it was brought into the kitchen to be killed. I would feverishly watch as it was clamped between the knees of one of the men. With one hand the man would hold back the wings, while another man would pluck the fine neck feathers from a small area. Each motion was resolute, precise. A small area of pink on the duck's neck would grow larger and larger with each jerk of the hand, like a multiplying organism. The throb on the patch of duck skin would be fierce and ready to bounce out rolling onto the floor. After the patch was clean, a sharp blade would be produced and a small white china bowl would be held in place. Then, with one swift slice, the duck's neck would be cut, the blood draining directly into the bowl, bubbles forming on top. The blood would be evenly poured into and shared among a number of plates. Lemon, mint, peanuts and pepper were sprinkled on top just as the blood began to congeal. Then the duck was plucked, cleaned and quickly boiled. Its flesh was used as broth for the rice porridge. The science was all in the timing. The scene could not be complete without lots of women running around, fussing, chopping and gossiping. The men, meanwhile, stood around talking about the size of the duck, which farm to go to, the best part of the neck to slice, and when and where they'd had the best congealed blood duck salad in Vietnam.

At the time, as the blood oozed from the live animal, I somehow did not register that it was in fact bleeding to death. Maybe I expected more sound. More flapping. More resistance. But towards the end of the duck's life, it seemed calm, resigned to its fate. As a child, this act of submission in the face of killing and annihilation seemed somehow natural.

After the food had been prepared, the familiar blue plastic sheet would be taken out again and unfolded in the backyard. It became a reliable old friend who, over the years, would come to bear witness to trails of beaming banter, silently recording the gradual weariness of these men, these story keepers. The beer cans would form a symphony of mixed song and the garden sprites of Bee-chump Street would tumble out of their roots to whiff at the commotion.

Growing up, my father seemed quite remote to me; a functional character who was head of the household, he existed mostly to provide and enforce rules. On these fleeting drunken occasions, though, I would catch glimpses of a spirit long buried. My yearning to be held by this spirit, to be nurtured by him, to know and understand him, was only compounded by his stoic character. My concept of my father over the years was a tapestry of these drunken, vulnerable and precious moments when he would tell stories of the old days of old Vietnam, and sing in French to me a lullaby that his father sang to him—a song sung from a child's point of view about his father's beautiful garden and all the lovely plants inside this space and time of freedom where all things flourished. My father would clap jovially in time with the vibrant backbeat of his song, sometimes still in his factory overalls and steel-capped boots. These glimpses gave me a brief view of the real man behind the father figure, and I longed to know and understand him. They were clues in my later search for his spirit, a search not for my father, but for a simple brave man before the heaviness of his world burdened him.

As the cans piled up, we would store them out the back near the garden. One by one I would place the empty cans on the concrete then jump on them to flatten each one into a compressed and uncompromising unit. Every few weeks, my father, Văn and I would go to the recycling spot near Punchbowl train station to trade in our formidable bags of beer cans for five cents a kilo. The huge recycling bins would tower above me like an austere school principal. I loved watching my father and Văn wrestle with the bags as the shiny compressed cans cascaded into a waterfall of aluminium. Given the number of bags, I'm surprised the Department of Family and Community Services wasn't called!

Each month, before the drinking properly began, the adults would gather in the living room to determine who would take out the loan kitty that month. At the point before my mother opened up each piece of folded paper, there would be a museum silence. The person with the lowest number would be announced and they would take out the cash loan that month.

Those were the happy times, monthly episodes of merriment. It was a time of optimism, too. My parents decided to build another house in the backyard in order to set up a larger garment-making operation with more machines employing more Vietnamese mothers.

At the time, I didn't fully understand the situation in Vietnam, but every so often my parents would bundle goods into boxes to be sent back home. Each box would contain everything imaginable for a long voyage: underwear, chopsticks, shirts, pens, soap. I would help put the goods in each box, inspecting everything to see whether there was something I could keep for myself. One time I saw a new T-shirt go into a box my uncle was preparing. It was turquoise with a cartoon drawing of a beach scene: a palm tree, orange sun and yellow sand. It even still had a tag. The shirt glowed with newness, infused with air-conditioning and fluorescent light from its time on a rack in a department store. Until the end of high school, most of my clothes were either second-hand or sewn by my mother. I almost salivated at the sight of this new T-shirt. Gently, my uncle explained that it was for Tiên, his youngest daughter in Vietnam. He promised he would buy me something else. It was the first time I realised my uncle's affection was divided, and the shock was numbing.

My parents would cover the boxes with unrelenting layers of poo-coloured tape. With my father's bold arched handwriting, he would write various addresses on the boxes, along with the names of my grandparents and my aunts. These names would float around in my head, but I didn't know where Gò Dầu, Tây Ninh province, Vietnam, was. Whether it had karate uniforms or kittens or secret berries or ducks with white feathers. I knew it was far away, though. With eight brothers and sisters on my mother's side and a few more on my father's side, as well as their spouses and children, all associated with the former disgraced regime, a lot of caring needed to be packaged.

•

When we moved to Punchbowl, I started school at St Jerome's Primary. I was immediately placed in the ESL class: English as a Second Language. I spoke Vietnamese at home and English outside. My parents knew the English jargon specific to their work and street-market vernacular—enough to get jobs done and discounted vegetables at the wholesale market in Flemington. Most likely the school had decided I needed assistance even without hearing me speak. I went to the classes for a few months, despite the fact that my English was fluent.

There was a Vietnamese man at the end of the street with a son the same age as me who also attended St Jerome's. I don't remember the son being in the ESL class though. Maybe because his dad had worn a tie at enrolment day. The man at the end of the street kindly drove me to school and picked me up every day. He had a considerable beard, the first beard I had ever seen. (The second beard was on Father Stephen, who came to replace the elderly Father Bill at Punchbowl parish. Father Stephen said Father Bill went to retire in the hills. I wonder now whether this was his way of sugar-coating Father Bill's death. It would have been fine to me. Father Bill was slightly deaf and would yell. His head had scales and hosted random hairs. The moderate hump on his back seemed to grow bigger each time he leaned down to speak to someone. Anyway, Father Stephen's arrival was a few years later.) At the time, I didn't understand how our neighbour's beard stayed on his face. Was it glued on? It was a constant source of fascination.

One afternoon we had an early mark. Instead of waiting for the man and his son, I decided to walk home to surprise my mother. When I got home I thought I would increase the surprise by sneaking in the side entrance. There was a tall wooden fence blocking the side passageway. Not wanting to spoil the surprise and go in the front entrance, I decided to deftly and mischievously climb the fence with my blue St Jerome's bag still on my back. When I got to the top, I lifted one leg over to straddle the fence, but the weight of the bag shifted and I lost my balance. I plunged head first onto the cold, unforgiving concrete below. My right temple made contact and I heard clearly the sound of the collision—a combination of a high *bing* and solid *thump*.

Still intent on surprising my mother, I got up and silently entered the back door. When my mother saw me, she was indeed surprised. She forced me to lie down while she inspected my temple, which immediately bruised and became swollen like a plum. For the next week, she rolled a boiled egg over my head so that the egg could absorb the bruise. The bruise went away but the bump didn't. It's a permanent reminder of my reckless fearlessness and a trace of my mother's ability just to keep going, even when it hurts.

•

My mother was pregnant. The pregnancy was fine but, as usual, my mother worked very hard. Australia's bicentennial year—celebrating two hundred years since the arrival of the First Fleet—drew to a close and 1989 dawned. The baby wasn't due for three months, but my mother went into labour. The baby was lying horizontally in my mother's womb and had to be delivered by caesarean. My baby brother, Vinh, was lifted out of my mother's belly, wrapped in a translucent film, uncrying, eyes closed. He weighed 1.3 kilograms and was immediately placed in an incubator at Bankstown hospital, about a fifteen-minute drive from our house. He would live there for the next three months. My mother believed he was a precious creature sent to her from the heavens.

Several times we would be called to the hospital in the middle of the night because his heart had stopped beating. The nurses asked my mother whether we would like to invite a spiritual leader to attend because it was possible death was imminent. A priest was called and he and my mother prayed together. My mother came home on one of these nights, kneeled down in front of the altar in our home, which had a picture of my deceased paternal grandfather on one side, the Virgin Mary in the centre, both beneath a crucifix which hung politely on a nail. She decided to strike a bargain with God, the Asian way. She would be prepared to lose all her money, all her material possessions, if only she was allowed to keep her son, this delicate fragile gift. That night she had a dream. A man dressed as a priest came to her and said that he had chased away all the demons lurking about ready to take Vinh away. The priest said that Vinh would now be safe. After that night, when the bargain was struck and she awoke from the dream, Vinh's heart never stopped beating again.

As I entered the hospital with my mother to visit Vinh a few weeks after he was born, I held onto the huge drawing I had made which was to be hung from Vinh's incubator. It was of Vinh as a superhero with a V stamped on a crest emblazoned across his chest. The colourful picture was drawn on a sheet torn from an industrial-sized roll of paper, given to us by a friend of my father's who worked in a paper factory. On one side, the paper was covered with a slight wax. The other had a rougher texture that made pencil marks bolder. As I scurried down the sanitised linoleum-covered hallway towards the baby unit, I held the long picture up high so it would not drag on the floor. The translucent paper flapped, hugging my body. When we arrived at the ward and I saw Vinh from across the room, he seemed to me like a mythical being that had fallen out of an epic poem, but stripped of his magical powers and needing to be nursed in the human world. His tiny body was sprouting tubes and covered in tape.

When we drew close to his incubator, my mother tapped on the glass ever so softly like a flake of falling sunlight. 'Vinh, it's Mummy.' Timidly, like a little fairy, Vinh opened his eyes. My mother asked whether I would like to hold him. A nurse took him out of the glass case, an uncrying lump of stillness, and placed him in my nine-year-old arms. From that extraordinary moment on, Vinh became the most precious thing in the world to me.

For years after, I would watch over him as he grew into a young man full of unusual wisdom and integrity, with a bewitching sense of wonder about the world. As my parents busied themselves on factory floors, sitting at sewing machines, making care packages and struggling to keep us in Catholic schools, I would attend to Vinh. I would be covered in a choking helplessness as I watched him sleep, struggling to breathe, his body fighting with asthma. At fourteen years old, I took him to St Jerome's on his first day of school. I cried as I watched him disappear into the line of grey shorts and blue shirts. At fifteen, I sewed him a Robin Hood costume with a cardboard feather taped on his hat for the Easter parade. I made him a bunny hat with chocolate eggs wrapped in gold foil inserted inside the top with cottonwool glued to the bunny's cheeks and ears. As a teenager, I was crippled with pain when I realised he was bullied in second grade by a red-headed bully by the name of George. I drafted a firm lawyer-like letter to the school which I later discovered was passed around the staffroom. They didn't believe it came from a fifteen-year-old. The bullying stopped.

Together we practised tying shoelaces, counting and reading. When it was time for his Holy Communion, I joined the parents' preparation committee, attending meetings in the church after school, still in my high school uniform. I met all his teachers from primary to high school; in all his years of schooling, I missed only one parent–teacher meeting. I discussed his academic progress with his teachers and areas in which he could do better, translating for my parents when they were able to come to the meetings too.

When he got to senior year in high school, the fees became far too expensive for us to manage. I wrote letters to the school asking for assistance, which they kindly gave. I attended his Friday night debating competitions. One week, after seeing his team lose narrowly, I asked the debating teacher, who seemed to have long ago given up on this B team, whether I could coach them for a session. One evening, over pizza at Vinh's friend's house, we dissected the mechanics of oral persuasion and argument. Although they didn't achieve a Hollywood-type turnaround, they improved markedly. When I attended his high school graduation ceremony at Bankstown sports club, I reflected on that day when, as a nine-year-old child, I'd first held him in my arms, his fragile heartbeat full of promise, and sensed that he was full of all that was good and pure in the world.

•

The community that my parents created became the very dagger that shredded and unravelled their Stitched-Together-Patchworkof-Possibilities. My mother had introduced a young woman to the money-lending syndicate who was a lovely sweet thing. In Vietnam, my grandmother had looked after this woman and her brother during their schooling as their parents did not have enough money to feed them. My mother called them her brother and sister. This lovely sweet thing fell in love with Duy, a recent arrival. He had left behind a family in Vietnam with a promise: one day, somehow, they would be reunited. In Australia he began a relationship with the sweet thing. She asked my mother whether Duy could join the syndicate. Although wary of his piercing eyes and syrup-like charm, my mother agreed. And so Duy joined the monthly ritual, drinking beer with the rest of the men and lavishing attention on the children which their own parents often could not.

At one unremarkable meeting of the syndicate, Duy wrote his number on the blue-lined scrap of paper, folded it and placed it in line with the others. It mocked my mother, daring her to expose its owner. My mother tells me that at that time, she knew. Her bones whispered loudly to her that sooner or later Duy would run. As he collected $15,000 and walked out the door that day, he glanced at her. His stare and her look were momentarily suspended in a magnetic field of knowing. He knew that she knew. Ever graceful, she returned to the merriment and continued to eat and laugh with the others, her cheeks flushing underneath the dermis, full of the heaviness of the Knowing, unsure how to tell my father he robbed us.

Incidents like this happened twice more. Though smaller amounts, they all added up to tens of thousands of dollars. One man who stole from us had gorgeous twin babies. He took the money and fled interstate. Later we would read in the community newspaper that he had been hailed as a hero for rescuing a child from certain death. It helped me to understand how grey the world really was, that situations and people didn't fit neatly into discrete categories of good and bad. That the matrix of decision making is driven by the power of circumstances. That behaviour does not necessarily reflect the essence of a person, and bad decisions can be born out of desperate circumstances. But at the time of the syndicate, as a child, I was far less sophisticated and forgiving.

In the 1980s, for a factory worker and his sweatshop wife, with three children and an extended web of family in Vietnam, all of whom depended on the money and goods that were sent home, the debt seemed insurmountable. People who knew of our crippling financial debacle showed my parents how they could both work and receive social security benefits. They could fake a divorce because single-mother allowances were much better than unemployment benefits, they suggested. Or my father could seek a psychiatrist and lodge a claim with veteran's affairs for an early Vietnam War veteran pension. But my parents' response to all such schemes was the same. My father told us that this was tantamount to stealing. It was cheating. It didn't matter whether the source of the money was a government, a corporation, your employer or your sister: if you did not earn it honestly, it did not belong to you. The government might not know, but you would and your children would. Karma can be dangerous. My mother agreed. She would have been unable to set our moral compasses if her own was defective. There were many times I would find my parents' stringent moral code frustrating and unaccommodating for the various grey circumstances in the world's societal abyss. I would see my mother's worldview as elementary and naive. Later, when I studied law and political philosophy, I would examine the intricate concepts of justice and rights set out by philosophers such as Kant, Weber and Rawls. But as I matured, travelled and lived through my own challenges, it was my parents' code, ebbing and swelling in my veins, smeared on my eyelids and pasted onto my voice from the chamber of my chest, that gave me my map for life.

The coordinators of a money-lending syndicate can choose to not pay back the members on behalf of the defaulter. In fact, that is what most syndicate coordinators choose to do. But not my parents. Members invested their money. Risk, borne by my parents, was theoretically thinly spread because of the associations of members—to my parents and to each other. It was an interdependent order of mutual opportunity and benefit, governed by Vietnamese, familial and human rules of trust. When my parents had decided to accept Duy into the syndicate, my parents reasoned they were accountable to the members.

Later, when I was old enough, I asked my parents why they didn't just tell the other syndicate members to each go after Duy for their cash. This was not unheard of; there were even organised gangs who hunted syndicate defaulters. But I learned that the members placed their trust in my parents because they were worthy of respect. They were worthy of respect because they had integrity. It was another illustration of the code. My mother had made a pact with God, she reminded me; she had been willing to trade all that she had for Vinh's life. What we were to lose was only money, only impermanent possessions. There are far more important things in life. Things that could make your heart ache and things that could make your soul weep with joy. The most important legacy you could leave your children was how you chose to live your life: the legacy of a good name and a moral code that lived in every unspoken gift-wrapped word given to strangers, from a dried mandarin from a gentle old tailor to a sarong from a Cambodian man. In time it was all supposed to come to me.

'Good things happen to good people,' my mother counselled.

'But the happening of the good things takes so long.'

'Everything will come if it is meant to. Trust me.'

No matter how my mother rationalised her actions at the time, with the debt that Duy and the others left, the community melody that had once bounced had become split. It fractured, blending into a flat black tone until it was a big Nothing. The big Nothing left a wound that for years and years frayed at the edge of my father's consciousness. Another wound to slip into his album which clung to his knees and fingertips like pollen.

To pay back everyone in the syndicate, my parents sought personal bank loans. A recession hit the economy, and interest rates began to escalate and compound like persistent layers of soot. My mother, grim-faced and pale, sat in numerous bank offices in petrified silence, uncertain as to whether the loans would be granted. She sewed day and night in the newly constructed house and workshop in the backyard while tending to her newborn baby. Suns, stars, moons and skies blended together into a whirl of machine pedals and fine fabric residue.

My parents had planned for a long time to bring my maternal grandparents and my paternal grandmother over to Australia for a visit. In the middle of all their troubles, the visit could not have happened at a more distressing time. Vietnam was still struggling with the legacy of Communist reforms, on the cusp of opening up to the rest of the world. It was unusual for ordinary Vietnamese people to travel overseas at the time, much less those who were old. A bus had been hired to carry forty or so of my relatives out to the airport some sixty kilometres away from Gò Dầu to see off my grandparents. My parents did not want to alarm their families about the financial situation. Rather than cancel the planned visit, they donned masks of contentment and welcomed my grandparents to Australia. They were to stay for a few months.

It was bizarre to have grandparents suddenly. Văn and I found it amusing to introduce them to western ways. When a burger from McDonald's was brought home for my grandfather, he unpacked all the bits on a plate. With a knife and fork he slowly tackled the beef patty, the lettuce, tomato, pickles, onion and buns. The bits had been separated onto the plate like a surrealist painting. My grandfather, still with dark blotches in his greying hair, was in his seventies. He dressed in a safari suit and fedora hat and used French words to describe beer and drivers. As I sat watching him eat, I did not appreciate that he had been imprisoned as a French resistance fighter, lived through two wars and outlived his eldest and youngest sons.

One evening, when my mother and father were out delivering a load of finished garments, Vinh—recently brought home from hospital—began to cry incessantly. I told my grandmother that he usually fell asleep whenever he was lying in his capsule in the car. So we took out the baby capsule and Grandma and I took it in turns to push Vinh up and down the short hallway, trying to simulate automobile motion. I made car noises. Grandma sang a Vietnamese lullaby. My mother walked in on this absurd scene, unsure of how to react. She finally chuckled when we all realised that it had worked. Vinh had stopped crying.

We took my grandparents to get their portraits taken. Both my grandmothers wore traditional velvet dresses with floral patterns. My maternal grandmother sat on a Victorian daybed inside the photographer's studio with one leg crossed over the other, the white satin pants showing beneath the front flap of the traditional *áo dài* dress. In the portrait, she is looking tentatively into the camera, the hard, sacrificial life of a Vietnamese woman, borne with grace and humility, in her gaze. Years later, at her funeral, this portrait would be carried by the eldest son of her eldest son. It would sit on the altar of her descendants wherever they were in the world, spread across America, Australia and

Vietnam, so that this humble, tenacious matriarch could receive our wishes and soften our fears.

One day, my maternal grandmother overheard a telephone conversation my mother was having. My mother was desperate and trying to borrow money. My grandmother's heart was shattering as she heard the frazzled brokenness in her daughter's voice. The next day she told my mother she wanted to go back to Vietnam because it was too cold in Australia. But she secretly did not want to be an additional financial burden on her eldest and most loyal daughter, and she could not bear to witness her child's agony.

But not long after my grandparents went back to Vietnam, my grandmother got mouth cancer. With limited medicinal supplies in the countryside, one morphine injection cost $100 at the time—a considerable amount of money, especially in the late 1980s and early 1990s. Loans were taken out to pay back loans. We spiralled deeper and deeper into debt. Duy was still around. His wife and children had now been sponsored over. Despite it all, my parents would help his innocent family settle into this strange land, offering everything from simple kitchen utensils to furniture. I guess the memory of tough beginnings was still vivid. No matter what Duy had done, his wife and children did not deserve to suffer. My mother asked Duy to pay us back, no matter how slowly. He complained that he didn't have a job. Later, after he'd bought a two-storey house and a brand-new four-wheel drive, he still refused my mother's request to pay us back $50 a month. At the time, my mother, who others often labelled as unreasonably compassionate, offered him a job at our workshop. She would teach him to sew. She had borrowed money to purchase a set of new sewing machines in anticipation of setting up a large workshop together with Duy's agreement to participate. But finally when it was all set up, he declared that the arrangement was unsatisfactory to him. He didn't want to drive to our workshop every day. In one last act of insanity, my mother offered to loan him one of our sewing machines so he could work at home.

One day, Duy arrived at our house, sidling down the path into the workshop. My mother greeted him briefly then carried on with her work, quickly returning to one of the machines to sew. She had two thousand more shirts to finish before 7 pm. The clock on the wall towered over her, its numbers and hands ready to fall out and surrender to Fractured Stress in the air. Duy began to dismantle one of the machines. As always, he was cloaked in a sickening sense of entitlement. I stood watching him resentfully. These were *our* machines. I knew that my father wasn't supposed to know about this ludicrous arrangement. My mother's rationale was that if we provided him with the means, there would be a chance we could recover a tiny fraction of what was due. Anything mattered to my mother at that point. But as a child, I saw only Duy's disgusting slyness paraded on his shoulders. It pranced ostentatiously down to the hollow of his cheeks and in and out of his chest and mouth. When I saw him at our precious machine, I ran as fast as I could along the red-brick path outside the workshop, up the concrete stairs leading to the front house, past the toilet and into the mustard-brown-tiled living room.

'Dad, he's taking our machine!'

My father, though confused, leaped up from the lounge and ran down the stairs and across the yard into the workshop. The next few moments are blurry. When my father saw what was happening, an insidious pain pierced his stomach as though a butterfly knife had been wedged into him. Clutching his side, he collapsed onto the floor like a soiled rag. Unsurprisingly, Duy cowardly fled the scene. My father was taken to hospital. The Fractured Stress had infused itself into his body, planting ulcers in his stomach. Now they had ruptured in a violent, vicious implosion. He had to be nursed through the next few months with bland rice porridge and extra gentleness.

My mother still sewed relentlessly each night. Each day. With eyes open. And sometimes with eyes closed. On one weekday lunchtime, she went into the bank. It was filled with collars, ties and overalls, all trying to squeeze in their banking during the break. My mother waited patiently in line for forty-five minutes. When she got to the teller, she handed in the withdrawal slip. It unmistakably and undeniably read $5. She never forgot the look on the young teller's face. Probably a girl in a summer job saving up for a holiday or new pairs of shoes. My mother walked out of the bank with her last $5. She made decisive, purposeful steps towards the bakery. The money was enough to purchase bread and a spread for her children's lunch that week. When she got home, my mother spent the next hour on her hands and knees, looking into every crevice of the house, behind every object, in the hope of a lost coin. The coolness of the mustard-brown-tiled floor kissed her cheeks softly, sadly, and the house cried silent tears of pity.

At that time, Uncle Căng's wife and three daughters had been sponsored over to Australia. They lived with us temporarily in our house and workshop in the backyard. My mother taught my newly arrived aunt to sew. But it wasn't enough. The piles of garments accumulated with each missed deadline. So did the debt. It rose like an uncharted mountain range, soaring into the stratosphere.

In 1990 we lost our beloved house. The FOR SALE sign came and went. The happy times faded into the empty cool space underneath our house, in between floor and earth where the mother cat had her litter. There were to be no more Monkey Magic games. No more handfuls of the first fruits of the season. No more sneaking through fence palings into the neighbour's yard for berries.

Our slice of the Australian dream was shattered and was to be sprinkled all over our modest footprints from Perth to Villawood to Newtown to Marrickville to Punchbowl. My family and I would become nomadic squatters destined to borrow a piece of someone else's dream in someone else's play. It was an open wound that hurt us all very deeply.

Uncle Căng and his family had recently rented a house in Punchbowl, a minute away from St Jerome's Primary School. It was an old white home, which would eventually be painted a new white with a green trim. An inappropriate minty impression that needed a snow-capped mountain and pine trees amid the suburban vista.

When our house was finally sold, we had nowhere to go. Now it was our turn to live with Uncle Căng and his family. Our haphazard belongings were packed into boxes which were strewn across the garage and rumpus room. My father, mother, Văn, Vinh and I all squeezed into a three-by-two-metre room, just large enough to fit my parents' king-size bed. That night, we all tried to sleep. I lay awake in bed, my father's snoring sending tremors into the springs of the mattress. With heightened alertness, I explored the sounds that hid inside the bones and green carpets of this unfamiliar house. I was alert to the webs on the windows, the coolness of the walls and my mother's nervous but regular breathing. This was our new home.

When my grandmother had visited in 1989, all her children owned houses except Uncle Căng. One of her last wishes was for Uncle Căng to be a homeowner. Whether it was a fifty-year-old wooden house built on a riverbank in Tây Ninh, or a fibro duplex in Bankstown, she craved for him the safety of a physical space to which he could always return—an uninterrupted and tangible creation of home, of safety. Title to a house meant you had the chance to create a past and a future. A set of memories nursed through hope, recession, fevers and graduation with walled photos that you could pass down to your children and their children. A place where your spirit could reside and where the custodians of your lineage could rest. Home was house. House was home. We had lost ours, but my relatives in Vietnam still did not know. As my grandmother lay dying of cancer, my dutiful, beautiful mother decided to grant my grandmother her final wish. It would be a gesture of gratitude and love to honour an exemplary woman who had suffered lifetimes of sacrifice.

With the money from the sale of our Beauchamp Street house, we paid off most of our debt. With most of the money we had left over, we could have put down a deposit on a new house or maybe started a small business. But instead, my mother provided Uncle Căng and his wife with a deposit to purchase their own slice of the Australian dream. I remember attending the house inspection with him, unaware that for the rest of their time in Australia, while his family would be settled, my family would be left to shift from one rented house to another.

The place my uncle eventually bought was a lovely fibro house with a decent-sized front yard and large backyard. In the front yard, on either side of the concrete path leading to the front door, were two Australian marsupials—a lifelike stone kangaroo and koala staring out onto the road like gentle protectors. All that was missing was an Australian flag in their paws. Inside the house, my uncle had a mirror he'd found at a garage sale, a souvenir from the 1983 Sydney to Hobart yacht race. A faux-mahogany display cabinet containing glass and porcelain kitsch from St Vinnies sat near the lounge. My uncle and his family's adoption of Australia as home had officially begun.

Over the years, the fibro house and Australian stone fauna would greet streams of Vietnamese refugees from my uncle's factory. Machine operators, forklift drivers and leading hands moving in and out of the house's passageways, carried by drunken tides of Vietnamese song. I would watch with bitter envy as my newly arrived cousins revelled in the familiar happy sounds of song and banter on cheap blue plastic every weekend. That innocent pleasure was lost to me.

CHAPTER 5

A maiden journey

School at St Jerome's went on as usual despite our changed circumstances. But my daydreaming flourished the more it seemed that the world was against us. As I watched Australian television, I dreamed of being someone with blonde hair and blue eyes—definitely not Vietnamese and not living in our cheap rented house in Punchbowl. Văn went to school and rarely shared any problems he faced. But alone he dealt with racist bullies and his own struggle for a place in the world. Somehow I am sure my mother knew of our angst and discontent.

By now it had been over a decade since my parents touched the earth which grew their families' rice. Over a decade since my mother had looked upon the Vàm Cỏ Đông River which passed through Gò Dầu, that had almost consumed her as a small child and whose banks sustained the house she was born in. When I was eleven years old, my mother decided to use the rest of the little money left after we had sold our house and after the mortgage deposit for my uncle to take her children back to the country where she was born. (My father couldn't come with us as the factory wouldn't give him the time off.) The three of us, born in three different countries, needed to know the Vietnamese meaning of family, of heritage, of identity. In Vietnamese, the concept of origin is—a blend of country and home—literally translated as 'earth water'. In 1991, we would spend five weeks in Vietnam.

We went to the Punchbowl post office to fill out applications for passports. When we finally received them, I examined mine. Under *Nationality* was typed *Australian*. I was baffled. I'd always thought I was Vietnamese. I didn't understand why it said Australian in my passport. My birthplace, ethnicity and nationality are all different, and for a long time I could not distinguish between these concepts. Even now, I hesitate when people ask where I am from.

In July, my mother accompanied her three children on their maiden journey to the mystical land of her childhood. On the day we left I wore a sky-blue collared shirt with a yellow knit jumper over the top. My jumper had diamond-like lattices all over it with ridiculous pompoms evenly positioned on my eleven-year-old torso. What was most significant was that for this special occasion, I had been allowed to purchase a brand-new jumper from a rack in Kmart.

We flew Qantas, the four of us sitting in the middle row. The plane seemed like it was a flying warehouse. Vinh was two years old and a very good passenger. He was dressed in a puzzle of scraps my mother had sewn from excess fabric. His pants had a Christmas cartoon motif while his T-shirt was layered with some black and yellow surf graphic. On the top he had a lamb's wool vest with light blue trim that had been given as a gift on his first birthday by a friend of my father's—he was definitely not dressed to be a calendar baby.

Tân Sơn Nhất airport in Ho Chi Minh City was substantially the same as it had been before the end of the Vietnam War. Both domestic and international flights and all passengers to Vietnam were processed inside its organs. I took a photo of my mother on the plane as she filled out our customs declaration and immigration cards. She is looking up at the camera abruptly as though interrupted mid-thought; her expression is anxious, oscillating between sure and unsure.

I remember stepping out of the plane onto the mobile staircase and being smacked by the dense humidity. We descended the steps and boarded the bus which would take us to the terminal. Vietnam had only embarked on its market-oriented reforms in 1986 and in 1991, there were still very few Vietnamese refugees returning to Vietnam for any reason. The US trade embargo had not yet been lifted. Fears of books of blacklisted escapees, a thousand watchful eyes and suspicions of persistent Communist persecution prevented many refugees from coming back. For those who did, the stories they told of regular requests to report to police coupled with impromptu inspections kept them nervously vigilant. These stories were delivered to inquisitive Vietnamese back in Australia who wondered whether Vietnam would ever be safe for them.

We had brought ten cartons of Eagle Brand medicated oil, highly prized even now for many people in the countryside. This green oil was used to cure every ailment on earth—rubbed on every part of the body that could feel. Under and on noses to clear nasal passages, on the temples for headaches, on stomachs to soothe indigestion and on the back during colds and flu. Each carton contained twenty-four bottles worth about $6 each. As we waited at the baggage carousel, my mother wore a sombre, reserved face. When we got our luggage, with poo-coloured tape on the outside (our names and addresses in Vietnam written in my father's arched handwriting), we realised our locks had been cut. On inspecting the bags, my mother discovered that two cartons of oil had been taken. At immigration, she slipped $20 into her passport, a clear expectation at the time. The sharp northern Vietnamese accent of the officer whipped at my mother, his eyes clearly inscribing the word *traitor* across my mother's forehead in slow precise script. Outside the airport, television screens transmitted images from inside the terminal to eager relatives outside. My relatives had hired a videographer to film the event on a huge VHS video recorder. This videographer would accompany us for the five weeks in Vietnam: to the Saigon zoo, on boats on the Vàm Cỏ Đông River and tending to ducks in my family's rice fields in the rain. He had a Tom Selleck moustache and kindred, lustrous eyes. Outside the airport, he filmed my mother on the television screen, scurrying about inside the belly of Tân Sơn Nhất. He then cut to my aunts, who pointed frantically at the screen bellowing, 'There she is! That's her! I swear! She's so fat!'

Finally, we glided out of the automatic doors. I hid behind the handle of the baggage trolley, suddenly shy. There seemed to be hundreds of people bunched up in rows folded into each other, pressed against the shiny railing that separated traveller from provincial relative, all rapidly scanning the exiting passengers for their separated kin. They all looked like me. All these strangers.

When my relatives and grandparents finally identified us, there was an onslaught of grabbing, screaming, crying and sniff-kissing—hugs, love, pity, warmth, grossness and healing all entwined in a potent decisive sniff. Sniffs came from all directions, from all smells, all heights. Sniff, sniff, sniff. Looking up, I saw only shreds of ceiling as I was swarmed by videographer, familiar grandparents and unfamiliar Vietnamese cousins. Still, the thick Saigon air buffeted my body, lifting me up above the noise and excitement.

We climbed aboard the hired bus and headed back to Gò Dầu village, Tây Ninh province, where She began. When we got to my grandfather's wooden house on the riverbank, it was dark. Neighbours lined the dirt-covered street. Bashful little boys, sucking on fingers and sugarcane, ran about, revelling in the celebratory atmosphere and senseless jolly. Those whom my mother remembered only as young sweet girls when she'd left on that fateful evening now brought out their children and even grandchildren to catch a glimpse of us: the returned spectacles.

My grandfather's house was full of yet more relatives who'd been unable to fit on the bus. They had come from the surrounding hamlets, communes and rice fields to welcome us with an immense feast. Knowing how much my mother loves durian fruit, my grandmother had one on hand and split it open as soon as we walked in the door. My mother beamed with happiness as the pungent, creamy, sugary odour filled the air and infiltrated the mellowed wood and stoked my mother's happiness. She was home.

•

The first thing we had to do when the sun came up was pay respect to our ancestors. We attended the gravesites of my mother's grandparents and gravesites on my father's side, buried on the land of their fathers and forefathers. We brought offerings of fruit, flowers, steamed dense sheets of rice noodle and roasted duck. Special leaves of paper money were burned so that the ancestors had enough to spend in the afterlife. Hell money, it's called, even though we don't know whether they are in heaven, hell or reincarnated. These days, loving descendants can also purchase paper houses, shirts, sports cars and iPhones.

At the gravesites, we all lit incense sticks, held them close to our hearts and heads, and then bowed three times. Once for the Creator, once for our ancestors and once for 'earth water'. At least that was how I understood it. Vinh stayed close to our mother, watching the ceremonies cautiously, clinging tightly to her leg. Seeing how shabbily dressed we all were, clad in dizzying collections of garments cobbled together out of leftover fabric from my mother's work, my aunts insisted that we all be measured for new clothes. We ended up with lovely tweed-patterned dresses, fine black trousers and respectable, almost regal shirts. Văn got a bronze and gold shimmering collared shirt which I believe he wore only once back in Australia—for a photo. It would have been a hit at Mardi Gras. When we returned to Sydney, my mother's grand new threads would end up in the bottom drawer, being inappropriate for a simple outworker to wear other than to large public Catholic celebrations.

For the next five weeks, everywhere we went, we were shadowed by a posse of our relatives. The group included my father's grown nieces and nephews from my aunt's fifteen children, and their children as well as various other relatives. I had no idea where they all fitted in the family tree. We spent most of the time in the countryside, visiting family, old great-aunts, second cousins and poor neighbours. Most received a green bottle of Eagle Brand oil, my mother's well wishes and her children's apprehensive smiles. We walked through bamboo groves to mud houses where grey-haired men in blue shorts slept on wooden beds. I would watch my mother's cousin climb a coconut tree with a machete to bring us fresh coconuts to drink. These were the special kind, naturally carbonated. The sizeable green ball rested on my lap as I sipped its sweet gassy goodness. With no flush toilets around, when I had to go my mother asked one of her cousins to take me to where I could do my business. I was led to a small plantation of tall bamboo and directed to just go anywhere. As I squatted on the ground, I noticed the sea of mutated fire ants. These were the largest ants I had ever seen in real life. I came back with souvenirs of itchy red marks on my bottom.

The humidity made my scaly eczema even more uncomfortable than usual. I tried mightily to not scratch but the dust, the heat and the excitement aggravated it. I dug at select bumps on the insides of my elbows and knees with my fingernails. This was in lieu of scratching the whole terrain. The indents from my fingernails into the few bumps provided only temporary relief. Unable to resist the sinister itch, I scratched until I bled. In addition to the eczema I occasionally suffered from asthma. Back in Australia, my mother boiled up a black bitter herbal medicine in a clay pot. To gather the ingredients, I went to Cabramatta, a suburb with many Vietnamese families, to the housing commission flat of an old man with a long white beard. He gave me various leaves and roots along with dried cicadas specifically to treat my asthma, but for some reason my dermis issues were never treated.

In Australia, my eczema caused me great trouble. I wanted to wear short denim overalls with a blue gingham cotton shirt inspired by Elly May Clampett of *The Beverly Hillbillies*. (Luckily, my ambitions later in life far more than compensated for this aesthetic childhood dream.) But my skin condition didn't allow such pleasures. To hide the wretched reptilian scales of eczema, even in summer I would ludicrously wear a jacket and pull my Sisters of St Joseph long brown socks far above my knees. My teacher and fellow pupils wondered what was wrong as sweat oozed from every pore of my body. 'I'm fine,' I would say casually as though *they* were the crazy ones. 'Let's keep playing.' I would concoct some way of distracting them—deliberately messing with the score of whatever game we were playing or walking backwards. Once, when the elastic of my sock was so worn that it slipped below my knee, I spent recess standing on one leg. When my friends asked what I was doing, I replied, 'I am standing on one leg. Obviously.' I rolled my eyes as though they were imbeciles. When the bell rang, I ran as fast as I could back to the classroom. Because Catholic school uniform socks were very expensive and not sold at the second-hand shop, I had to improvise by placing rubber bands around the outside of my socks and then folding them down over the top. The trick worked but I would come home with a deep purple ring around my leg as though I had been sliced by a sickle. At the time I was terribly despondent. I envied girls who wore dresses and walked around itch-free.

When my grandmother saw the curse that was clinging to me, she prepared her elimination method. Horse dung. Steamed. I lay over a bamboo bed while the fumes from the dried horse dung wafted through the cracks of the bamboo and into my skin. At least, this is what my mother tells me happened; I absolutely have no recollection of the procedure. Maybe I purged the experience from my memory. It's not something that one likes to recount to others. But whether it really was the horse dung, or puberty or utter humiliation, the reptilian disease never returned.

•

Within a couple of weeks of our arrival, my mother's two eldest brothers and their families were to move to America under a humanitarian scheme for Southern Vietnamese officers of particular rank. My mother's eldest brother had suffered greatly in the re-education camp after the war ended. Giant rats had gnawed at his leg and the untreated wound left him with a permanent injury. The subsequent limp followed him to the great land of America and would turn into a haunting reminder of dark, dark times. The organisation sponsoring my uncles was a Lutheran church in Colorado. Pueblo and Boulder in Colorado would become their home. It was 1991 and not many Vietnamese had successfully emigrated to America under the humanitarian scheme. Buses filled with our relatives and my cousin's friends travelled to the airport to say goodbye. Clad in my new tweed pinafore, a white blouse and white Kmart shoes, I held onto my nine-year-old cousin Anh. I had no reason to sob really. But I did. It was all on camera. My older teen cousins received carefully folded love letters from friends who'd never had the courage to declare their feelings. Hopes of long-distance bonds were harboured. Teenage hearts that were left behind in the small village of Gò Dầu would forever live in this moment of goodbye, a moment on the cusp of where their worlds would diverge forever. It was in this last moment that they and my cousins would be the same. Of the same village, the same childhood games of chopsticks and marbles, the same school, the same struggles. Over a decade later, my cousins would return with university degrees, their American-born husbands and English-speaking children. They would look upon their friends from the airport that day in 1991, now selling fabric in the dim narrow aisles of the Gò Dầu market, or with hands callused from fixing Honda motorbikes and hearts worn from nursing flailing love stories. But at the airport that day as my grandparents said goodbye to their sons and grandchildren, uncertainty wrapped itself around everyone. There were last glimpses. From friends, family and secret loves. Full of pensive anguish. Full of possibility.

A week or so after the Big Goodbye had found its place and settled in hearts, camera film and phone calls, we visited my mother's family's rice fields—the place where, after the fall of Saigon, she spent much time, back bent against the sun, planting, tending and cutting across seasons and sorrows. My aunts told us that my mother, her pants already soaked from being submerged in the wet ground, would squat without shame in the fields, piss in her pants, then keep on planting. Time and hope against her. I stood on the banks of earth separating the fields of dry stalks. The fields had just been hoed. Lovely white ducks skittishly waddled across the field and I chased them with a long bamboo stick, clomping through the wet earth, the shoots of cut rice stabbing my tender urban Australian feet. I watched the workers separating the grain from the stalks, streams of grain shooting out of the machine like a cascading shower of brown and yellow pixels. The men and women sifted the grains through a giant woven basket suspended from a skeletal bamboo frame. I attempted the task myself, the videographer filming my feeble, cumbersome efforts, much of which were staged for the camera.

On a cyclo, Vinh, my mother and I toured Ho Chi Minh City under the watchfulness of Tom Selleck, who later dubbed in the well-known upbeat song 'Sài Gòn đẹp lắm, Sài Gòn ơi!' (Saigon you are so beautiful, oh Saigon!') The cyclo cruised across District 1 of the city while the swarm of traffic swirled around us. The cyclo driver beamed into the viewfinder of the camera in front, relishing the rare chance at being in front of a camera. My mother recounted her memories of Saigon from when she studied there as a young woman. The narration continued past the main roundabout across Ben Thanh market, in front of the opera house and behind the cathedral, remnants from the French occupation.

Back in Gò Dầu, Văn, Vinh and I were exposed to uncensored village life, without luminous supermarkets, refrigerators or *Wheel of Fortune*. When Vinh wasn't being carried, he walked only on his tiptoes, the same way he walked in Paddy's Markets after he saw orange peel and rubbish on the ground. At the market, fish and eels would squirm inside aluminium buckets. Clumps of noisy ducks, roosters and chickens were heaped together on the ground. Balls of glutinous rice wrapped around yellow bean paste floated in buckets of ginger-infused syrup, spooned into small plastic bags with dollops of coconut milk and sesame.

The neighbours were preparing for a death anniversary celebration and had bought a cow. I stretched upwards above the ring of onlookers and managed to get a snapshot of the epicentre of the crowd. Inside the ring of the fervent audience was the live cow with its legs tied together. A man held a sharp rod linked to a cable which was connected to an electric socket in the wall. I ran into the house but still heard the thumps of the struggle and the sounds of slaughter. My grandmother told me that on one occasion she looked through a hole in the wall directly into the eye of a cow being slaughtered and saw tears streaming from its eye.

There are lots of photos from that first Vietnam trip. Numerous pictures of the extended family gathered under my patriarchal grandfather's wings. I am always in the front of the clan, hands by my side, standing to attention, clenching a smile to force out a dimple on my left cheek. A trick I learned in second grade.

On the day we left, I stood out the back of my grandfather's house gazing at the brown river, the continuous current carrying families on small boats, selling their vegetables up and down the river. I don't know why I cried, really. My five weeks could not have warranted a potent attachment to this place. My aunts chuckled at my melodramatic display. That morning, as on every other morning, the man down the street, shirtless and in blue shorts, brought us noodles with pork made from the slaughtered pigs whose monstrous squeals I had heard the night before. When I visited eight and sixteen years later, he would continue to bring me noodles, still wearing blue shorts, his bare torso like dark leather, always bearing a defiant shimmer.

We all clambered onto the rickety blue vehicle, a type of mini-truck owned by my grandfather's neighbour. The back tray of the truck had two rows of seats facing each other and was covered by a plastic roof. Passengers at the back could only look to the side of the truck or behind it, never ahead. I always wanted to sit at the edge of the row closest to the opening. We pulled away from my grandfather's house, the truck and its passengers bobbing as it struggled over the rocks and potholes on the dusty village road. Children from the neighbourhood followed behind. As my mother's childhood drifted past, we waved to all the characters who had become part of my story too. The noodle man in the blue shorts. The pigs ready for slaughter. The lady whose bad nose job left the bridge of her nose with a transparent glow on sunny days. Goodbye, wet season. Goodbye, jumping frogs. Goodbye, golden jackfruit bursting from their skins.

When we finally got up onto the tar road, the driver accelerated. The neighbourhood kids stopped chasing after us and began to wave. Just like in the midday movies but this time it was in full colour. They disappeared into figures, then shapeless things, then ragged dots of movement, then the horizon. The conversation around me became a sort of white noise. Muffled. Submerged. Unable to look ahead, I looked behind. Grey sheets of road rolled out behind us. Just enough road to surge ahead. We zoomed past women on bicycles with conical hats, men on

Honda motorbikes with roosters hanging off the bike like feather boas, past the stone business with its field of stone giraffes, elephants and tigers. Safaris of frozen haphazard bits of trapped life trailing after me. Goodbye, Vietnam.

•

Back in Sydney, there was a cavity where the extended family membrane of Commotion and Big Fuss, Big Sniffs, Big Love sat for five weeks. My misery was compounded as I discovered my class had learned long division while I was away. I found long division hard to master without someone demonstrating it. One day, I ran home from school in tears because I didn't understand what the class was doing. My mother purchased a series of tuition videos called *Maths Made Easy* from a Vietnamese acquaintance who was a door-to-door knowledge salesman occasionally dabbling as a translation services broker. He later would sell us both the children's and adult *World Book Encyclopaedia* for a substantial sum of money. (We paid extra for the gold glazing on the edges of the pages.) He would also later get me a certified English translation of my Thai birth certificate, which before then I could never read.

The cover of the maths video had a sketch of a happy boy with numbers prancing over his head. The long-division section of the video was taught by a man in cream pants and a blue shirt with a beard so tremendous the lesson came out as a series of mumbles. Needless to say I didn't focus on the maths but on the primal movement of the beard. I never properly mastered long division. Fortunately, the discovery of calculators would relieve my sense of inadequacy, at least in that regard.

•

We had continued to live in my uncle's old rented house after he had left for his newly purchased one. My mother and father set up the sewing workshop at the back of the rented house similar to the set up at the home we sold. We laid down light green plastic so the dust and thread wouldn't embed itself into the carpet. The carpet through most of the house was khaki green. I would stay in my little oasis at the back where my whole family had slept on our first night there. But I would miss my mother's skin. I would climb into bed with her. Sometimes she would still be wearing a bra. I liked running my fingernails along the tiny ribbing of the straps. She would have a cassette player near her head. It would play Vietnamese opera, always stories of longing, sadness, unrequited or forbidden love. She would cry herself to sleep to these painful but strangely soothing lullabies.

Our family's pockets were basically empty and it would continue to be a difficult journey for us. We couldn't afford a washing machine at the time. I remember being in the outside laundry one winter, washing the sheets by hand, the water bitterly cold and unforgiving. Like clockwork, early every Saturday morning my parents would head to Flemington markets where the produce was cheap and fresh. My mother would come to know all the Vietnamese vendors. Their kids would be sleeping under the tables, or selling cucumbers, competing with big-bellied Italian men with booming voices.

We had lovely neighbours. To the right was a Vietnamese family. They had a son who was Văn's age and would become one of Văn's oldest friends. To our right was a Greek family whose youngest daughter, Karissa, went to school with me. Occasionally I would be invited into their house. It seemed to me like a shrine to all things beautiful. The house smelled of fine precious things. Of rest.

One Christmas I was allowed to go over and play. I walked across the manicured front garden, up the stairs and into the hallway. The runner was soft beneath my awkward feet. The decorated Christmas tree had musical lights that echoed magical sounds like floating bells. There were wrapped, glistening presents underneath the tree. Framed mirrors and pictures adorned the walls. Lovely burgundy rugs were sprawled on the floor. There was a pool out the back and an open-plan kitchen. As I nervously gazed at it all, wide-eyed, I somehow felt that it was familiar, with its golden clocks, porcelain dolls and silver-trimmed glassware. I realised that this was a house I had pieced together from countless catalogues.

Our letterbox was routinely stuffed with junk mail, and I would gather the catalogues and retreat to my room. In a quiet space, I would lay them out, forensically examining each coloured page. Savouring worlds of dolls, garden gnomes, curtains, fold-out lounges, televisions and washing machines. I would ration the catalogues over a few days until the next batch. Items from

Freedom Furniture, Target, the Reject Shop and Harvey Norman would be circled with a pen as I slowly constructed our own shrine of Lovely Things. Very special items were cut out and kept in my top drawer.

Karissa had all the toys a little girl could wish for. We played with her Barbie dolls and doll's house in her room. Her father, grey-haired with a gentle smile, had worked hard in a factory all his life. As well as Karissa, he had a successful grown son and daughter, each married with kids. I knew when the grown daughter was visiting from affluent Hunters Hill. Her new E-class black Mercedes always announced her presence, like a black panther cruising past Western Sydney.

Behind us was a Lebanese family with four kids, one of whom was Vinh's age. The father was a train driver and the mother stayed at home. From the back fence she would pass over to me tabouli salad made from parsley that she grew in her yard. This mix of ethnicities was typical of Punchbowl, a suburb full of hard-working immigrant families just like ours. A place where diversity was inherent and struggle was second nature. South, east and west of us were families with broken English and working class origins. Each with their own dreams. Each in a different stage of the settlement process. All with kids the same age as my brothers and me at St Jerome's primary school. Karissa's family had emerged as the successful immigrant crew. They represented what could be. To our north was Rossmore Avenue, a street with a church on one end and on the other, Punchbowl Public

School and Canterbury Road, a couple of hundred metres from the known Canterbury Road prostitutes' strip.

In the heart of it all was our little unit. Just another family. For a long time, my father did the night shift at the F. Muller factory. When we woke, he was asleep. When he came home, we were at school. The Hard Yakka industrial uniform with steel-capped factory-issued boots became him. My mother would be at the sewing machine pedalling for school fees, for family assistance in Vietnam, for Telecom bills, for a way out.

•

One hot summer weekend, while my father was at work and my mother was sewing, I went out to the backyard and stood under the hose to cool down. Afterwards, I lay on the grass looking up at the clouds, trying to trace outlines of kings, elephants, trees, superheroes and crickets. I looked at the worn underwear hanging on the line, flapping like flattened jungle leaves from nature documentaries. It got late and my father had just come home from the factory. My parents had to deliver a load of garments. I was supposed to watch Vinh; they couldn't take him with them because the garments had filled the boot and the backseat. Văn was at tae kwon do practice at a community club in Lakemba, one suburb away.

Vinh was as attached to my mother as I was at his age. She had to sneak out of the house as she did over a decade earlier with another desperate child. This paused scene of stealth disappearance was replayed to her like a lost button that resurfaces again and again. When Vinh realised that my mother had left he began to cry. There was nothing I could do to stop him. It was an excruciating feeling. Helplessness engulfed me like a toxic gas. I tried to entertain him, making up stories about where our mother was. I took photographs of him so that he could pose and momentarily stop crying. I made him wear the Easter hat I had created for the school parade. Nothing worked. I felt like an exhausted circus performer.

As Vinh sat on the floor in the back room screaming, the grand sewing machines also wept. His ceaseless cries clung onto the dusty blinds and broken swing in the yard. I went back outside to lie on the ground, trying to block the piercing desperate screams, but it was impossible to recapture the carefree spirit of the afternoon. I felt completely and utterly helpless. For the first time in my life, I had the sensation that I was truly alone. There was no one to rescue me. No one to say everything would be alright. No one to take over the responsibility. That was supposed to be the job of my mother's youngest brother, lost somewhere in the jungles of Cambodia.

The emptiness of the house gnawed at my fingertips and toes. Feelings of infinite desperation unravelled and wrapped themselves around my eleven-year-old body while Vinh's screeching cries continued to deafen my small ears. When my parents eventually returned, the solemnity of adulthood had already seized me. It took away my freedom to play, to wonder. It would be years before the solemnity would let go.

CHAPTER 6

Why didn't you get 100?

Like most girls from St Jerome's, I went on to MacKillop Girls High School in Lakemba, right next door to St John's Boys High School. In the mornings, I would walk to Punchbowl train station and make the short trip through Wiley Park to Lakemba. Sometimes I would get a lift with Karissa in her mother's Mercedes. Often, when I needed to wait in their house, it gave me a chance to glimpse their precious things. We weren't friends at school. It wasn't even openly acknowledged that we were neighbours. The contrast of our families' socioeconomic status embarrassed me.

The transition to high school wasn't too troublesome, given that most of my primary school friends also enrolled at MacKillop Girls. The year I started high school, it was now my father's turn to visit Vietnam. At the time, my father did not indicate any reservations. But looking back, I can only imagine the deep trepidation he must have felt, returning to the country he had fled. At the airport, we said goodbye and I asked my father to bring me back a white teddy bear. Looking back, it was a silly request, no doubt fabricated from cheesy Hollywood movies. On his way back, the white bear would cause him problems at customs in Vietnam. They wanted to slice it open, suspecting that my father was trafficking drugs. Knowing his indelible fear of Vietnamese authorities, I cannot fathom what torture that experience must have been. Trying to contain the flood of memories of uniforms ruling his re-education camp life, grinding his dignity with abuse.

I had also asked my father to bring me back a pair of Reeboks to replace my cheap shoes from Best & Less, which were branded Apple Pie and Grizzly. He brought me back a pair of white high-tops with pink trim and embroidered logo. Perfect. At school everyone noticed my shoes straight away. It was obviously a model that was not available in Australia. A true import. But very quickly someone pointed out that my shoes had *Reobek* imprinted on them instead of *Reebok*. I was mortified. I was further punished the next day after I returned to wearing Apple Pies.

One weekend while my father was in Vietnam, the phone rang. I picked up the phone in the back room where the sewing machines were. My aunt's voice echoed down the line from Vietnam.

'Cat Thao, is that you? Is your mum home?'

'Yes, it's me. But Mum's not home now.'

'She's dead. Grandma's dead.'

I didn't know how to react over the phone. It seemed ridiculous and silly to me. So I chuckled. Out loud. The chuckle left me rude, uncensored. I said my mother would call back later and hung up. When my mother got home, I delivered the news to her swiftly and directly. A clean execution. I watched as she began to quietly tremble, the little tremors rippling through the cells in her body. The door remained open behind her. Her face collapsed with yet another blow of sorrow. Tears ran down her face. She called Vietnam straight away.

Not long after the phone calls, the garment contractor came by. He was a ferocious-looking Vietnamese man with bullock eyes that seemed on the verge of falling out of his head. His angular head sat uncomfortably on a tall, thin frame. His coarse sparse hair became wild when he spoke, as did his eyes. My mother asked whether she could return the half-completed load. Her mother had died and she would be unable to finish it with all the preparations in Vietnam and ceremonies to be done here.

'You have to finish the load by the deadline. People die all the time.'

My mother stared at him. His bullock eyes gazed back at her, unflinching. The sewing machines and I watched in swampy terrorized silence before the next words were uttered. The unfinished garments, half stitched, half happy, tried to retreat into themselves to hide from the towering male figure in the doorway. He hadn't even paid us yet for the last load. He would use this unpaid money as ransom, knowing how much we needed it. So my mother agreed to complete the load by the deadline. She rallied all her friends. They came over to help her where they could. She spent the nights alone at the machine, sobbing and sewing. Sobbing for her mother, for her children and the damned wretched destiny that imprisoned her in this way. But the more she sewed, blinded by a scorching heartache, the more we had to unstitch the garments. Lines of thread made their own trails across the fabric, skating to an unknown song, a thousand stitches long.

In Vietnam, my father did all he could to look after the funeral preparations and ceremonies. Even before any of the relatives had known of the death, my grandmother's sister-in-law had arrived at the house to help. My aunts asked her how she knew. She said, 'Your mother told me in my dream last night that she had died and that I was to come down and help you kids with all the arrangements.'

Every aspect of my grandmother's funeral was filmed so that my mother and her brothers in the US could know that the family in Vietnam had done all the proper things required and that the funeral was sufficiently large and well attended. Mental notes were taken of who was there and who wasn't. On the altar, the burnt ashes from incense sticks curled savagely without breaking off, a sign that ancestors and other spirits are present. My grandmother had hidden her gold somewhere in the house. To ensure that the coffin was not raided and the house kept sacred, the family set out to locate the gold. My grandmother's eyes remained open the whole time, even when my aunts tried to forced them shut. Bảo, her favourite grandchild, the eldest son of her eldest son, had returned from Colorado for a visit. She had died in his arms. Appropriately and rightfully, Bảo was the one who eventually found the hidden gold. Only then did my grandmother close her eyes. All the descendants were dressed in white and wore strips of white cloth tied around their foreheads. Bảo, as the eldest son of the eldest son, was identified by a single red dot on his white headband. Not even the eldest son himself has this privilege.

My grandmother's family practise Cao Đài. In the Holy See in the capital of Tây Ninh sits the first and prime temple of their religion. It is elaborately and brightly decorated. In it there is a statue of Jesus Christ as well as one of Mohammed. The French writer Victor Hugo is considered a saint and is charged with evangelising the west. Members of the Cao Đài faith in Australia raised funds to build a replica temple in Wiley Park in southwest Sydney. Wearing traditional Vietnamese dress, on weekends they would volunteer their time to lay bricks, paint or cook for the builders. The temple was completed over a period of ten years.

A three-day prayer ceremony for my grandmother was held at the incomplete Cao Đài temple in Wiley Park. My mother was dressed in a white cotton traditional dress and also wore a white cotton headband. Inside the lavishly decorated temple, upstairs where coloured dragons twisted upwards around thick columns, we kneeled on round embroidered pillows while the congregation chanted prayers for hours. The ringing sounds of brass gongs occasionally disturbed the air and reverberated against the omnipresent Asian 'One Eye' painted on a perfect giant solid sphere, decorated with the sky.

After my grandmother died, a portrait of her assumed a position on our altar, along with the Virgin Mary and my paternal grandfather. Every time we moved, the altar was the first thing to be packed and unpacked. On top of the tallest chest in a central space, usually the living room, my mother would lay out a blue piece of fabric. She would carefully place the statue of the Virgin Mary in the centre and position the pictures of my grandparents on either side of the statue. A vase of fresh flowers and fruit would also be placed at the altar. Whenever there was a death anniversary of an ancestor or an important date in the lunar calendar, we would place food that we had cooked at the altar for our ancestors. Only once we had finished offering our prayers with lit incense would we be permitted to eat. On these occasions, there would always be a cup of rice, salt and water—the staples of life. The altar grounded us. It was a connection to our forefathers, a constant reminder of who we were and where we had come from. Although the centrifugal forces of life pushed things outwards, no matter how far we were flung from the centre, this core remained unchanged. Our ancestors watched over us. Ate with us. Forgave us. Received our tears. Celebrated our joys. And dreamed with us.

My grandmother became my guardian. As the idea of organised religion and the political contradictions of the church disillusioned me, I talked to my grandmother. When I next visited

Vietnam, I brought home her traditional Southern Vietnamese pyjamas. They fitted me perfectly. I would often wear the black shirt with jeans. There were slits on either side for ventilation as the farmers worked in the sun. There were large pockets on either side of the snap buttons down the front. Together with jeans, it was my sartorial attempt to fuse east and west.

In Vietnam, people would go to the temple to search for answers. After a quiet prayer a question would be posed. Two small blocks of wood would be tossed. If the two blocks landed in a certain way the answer would be yes. In Australia, my mother improvised with two twenty-cent coins and a saucer. After praying to my grandmother at the altar and lighting incense, I would toss the coins. If heads and tails came up, the answer was yes. If it was a double heads or double tails then the answer was negative. Simple. I consulted my grandmother on many things, from whether I should defer university or take a particular job to whether or not the guy I was dating was my future husband. At night, before I went to sleep, I would make the sign of the cross (after years of Catholic education I couldn't quite give up the habit) then pray to my grandmother. She replaced the Father, the Son and the Holy Spirit. It was a somewhat confused hybrid of faith and worship.

•

As I was beginning high school, throughout Western Sydney there were fights between groups of Vietnamese and Lebanese kids. In hindsight it wasn't anything to do with gang activity or organised crime; more likely it was just about minority kids being territorial and defensive, trying to claim turf in an assertion of clan and community. The majority of Vietnamese refugees and Lebanese immigrants to Australia arrived at about the same time. We were different to the Greeks and Italians who were already largely settled. They had worked hard over generations to establish an economic and political presence in Australian society. They had money and they had a voice. All that we newer migrants had were fresh wounds and fear. We were living in rented houses whose front doors opened out onto a sweeping landscape of uncertainty. But we had each other. Our kind. My kind. People whose spices meant the same things. Whose food tasted the same, whose rituals were mirrored, whose silence was understood.

At various public and private schools in Western Sydney, fights were breaking out. Maybe it started independently at one or two schools but because of cousins and connections elsewhere, everyone was eventually dragged from one place to another for backup. For pride. For our people. At my all-girls school, a quiet Vietnamese student with broken English and a Demi-Moore-circa-*Ghost* haircut suddenly had enough of the fighting. The version I heard was that she was teased by a Lebanese student. This usually placid Vietnamese girl reacted. What started as bullying became reframed as a tribal battle: a battle to defend the honour of our people. Phone calls were made. Times arranged. Supporters rallied. At 3.30 pm one day, when Lakemba train station was packed with uniforms from MacKillop and St John's high schools, it was on. Apparently school compasses were used to stab people. I arrived late, after it was all over, but saw blood on a fellow student's uniform. The spots of blood on the baby blue shirt looked like the beginnings of a Jackson Pollock. Fortunately, it was someone else's blood that had splattered on her. She recounted the events to me. I later heard that Sefton and Chester Hill high schools had the same issues. Knives were brought to school. Then came police and sniffer dogs.

I don't know when it all died out. Maybe I stopped listening and seeing. Maybe we just grew up. Maybe our respective tribes became more settled and there was less to prove. Less to look back at what we had to defend and more to look ahead, to go forward.

At MacKillop I was a diligent student. I stayed up all night to memorise textbooks. I did not go to any parties and knew nothing of boys. Life was study leavened with rations of *Astro Boy*, *Transformers* and *Monkey Magic*. I always kept the top button of my shirt done up. The library was shared between the boys and girls high schools but it was located at St John's. I tried to avoid going to the library at lunchtime because it meant crossing the boys' playground – an utterly mortifying experience. If it was an urgent and pressing assignment, I would quickly power walk my way across the bitumen, head down, focusing on my footsteps. Boys, handballs, court lines flurried past my peripheral vision.

When the students had left for the day, I stayed after school in the library three days a week to get extra work done. I entered statewide mathematics and science competitions. One year I created a board game around Pythagoras' Theorem. I went to the hardware store to buy chipboard, brass hinges and screws, and made a coloured numbered spinner instead of dice. It was a simple concept: random questions around Pythagoras' Theorem had to be answered before the player could move. They had to reach the end of the squiggly series of coloured squares. There was a limit of four players. I won an award. Of course. I had to receive an award, even if it was for supreme nerdiness.

I was part of the debating team and always second speaker. I was not confident enough to open but was a little too egotistical to settle for summing up as third speaker. Second was where I felt comfortable. It was the position in the debate where you could really solidify the win or turn things around. Unless our school hosted, most of the time we had to travel to other schools each Friday night during debate season. My father would drop me off at the school and my English teacher, a feisty Greek Australian woman with dyed orange hair and worry lines between her eyebrows, drove me to the hosting school every week. My father would wait outside my school at about 9 or 10 pm to pick me up. Only once did a police officer question him for parking in the dark outside a school on a Friday night.

I think my parents only ever watched one debate. Even then they didn't understand what was being said, so there was really no point in them attending. They were busy working and trying to surmount all the obstacles I wasn't fully aware of at the time. We had an understanding. My job was to study hard, translate for them, deal with government authorities, banks and insurance providers, and look after Vinh.

In year eight, I came first in every subject except one, in which I came second. I don't know whether my parents understood what a feat this was. I had even come first in English and physical education. Although I was small, I was sufficiently agile to pass all the physical tasks. I was far more challenged than the broad-shouldered swimmer types but managed to overcompensate in the theory component. It really didn't matter how well I went at shot-put or javelin. I named all the sports in a decathlon as well as all the moves in floor gymnastics and the array of gymnastics equipment.

Ironically, the subject I came second in was Vietnamese. Apparently I couldn't be the best all of the time. Because of the number of Vietnamese- and Arabic-speaking students at the school, the school offered these languages in addition to the standard Italian and French. Vietnamese was taught by Ms Ngoc. She had a short bob and large plastic-rimmed glasses. She looked best when she wore a navy skirt with a white shirt that had large navy polka dots. She didn't have matching navy high heels but her black pointy closed-toe shoes were sufficient. Everyone in the class was of Vietnamese origin. In the Italian class there was a Vietnamese girl whose family had been resettled in Italy before moving to Australia. She spoke better Italian than the second-generation Italian kids.

I wrote lots of stories in Vietnamese class during those first couple of years of high school. My mother kept many of them.

There is a story about a girl who grows up, falls in love and gets married to a Vietnamese guy. She finds out that her husband and her father are the same type. In the story, I had written in Vietnamese 'men are all useless'. Some concepts transcend language and culture!

When I received ninety-nine per cent in a maths exam, my father asked me why I didn't get a hundred. When I came second in Vietnamese, he asked why I didn't come first, despite coming first in all the other subjects. It was a kind of tough love that confuses children growing up in a western society, where television parents regularly give unconditional hugs and tell their children, 'I love you'. Or where parents say, 'as long as you do your best'. Ludicrous. How can mediocrity ever be okay? I may not have had a Tiger Mum yelling at me, but the pressure was there. I was raised with the typical academic expectations of Asian children as reported on tabloid current affairs shows and caricatured by my fellow Australians on the ABC. But I didn't play the violin or piano; we couldn't afford the lessons. It might not be reasonable but the pressure to excel academically makes sense. As people who are physically smaller, we didn't have a real chance at being sports stars unless it was in table tennis, badminton or snooker. Maybe golf. But the cost of golf club memberships would exclude most refugees. The only legal way to attain financial security for families with no capital, no language and no political access was education.

As a kid, I understood this instinctively. Even as I meticulously decorated my year two weather project with glitter pen, I knew.

When my mother had a minor car accident with a Bankstown real estate agent when I was seven, I negotiated with him over the phone in English while my mother sat beside me nervously. When the landlady in Punchbowl berated my mother for not paying the rent on time or not keeping the kitchen clean, I translated. I watched as my mother stood silent in her attempt to retain her self-respect. I didn't know how to translate dignity. Or grace. My mind wasn't quick or brave enough to rebut the landlady on her behalf. All I could do was stand there, telling my mother off in Vietnamese for the landlady. A borrowed mouth of poison.

I had been trained in the language of responsibility and sacrifice. I was exposed to the intimate moments of quiet humiliation that accumulate like rust when a parent must rely on their small child to read medicine packaging, to fill out application forms. For grown-up things. And I knew that it was my job to study hard and succeed, to make my parents' years of sacrifice worthwhile—which meant that nothing could be allowed to disrupt my studies.

One day, I got off the train at Punchbowl station as usual and started walking home down Rossmore Avenue. Jessica Jones and her older sister Peta also got off at Punchbowl. Jessica was in the same year as me and we had gone to primary school together but weren't really friends. Jessica was a stocky girl with glossy blonde hair. Her sister was freckled and slender. She excelled in athletics. Their mother did shifts at the St Jerome's canteen and was probably head of the parents and teachers committee as well. When I bought twenty cents' worth of liquorice at the canteen,

I would politely say hello to Mrs Jones. I secretly daydreamed that my mother would also be behind the metal grilles, serving fellow pupils with a warm smile and keen eyes. I imagined my mother being an active member of the school community so that I would have some sort of respect in the classroom and playground. But that was never to be the case.

As I walked down Rossmore Avenue, I noticed that the Jones sisters were walking behind me. The air was crisp. It was sunny. The size and weight of my school bag was not commensurate to my fragile frame. I felt like a sea tortoise stranded in suburban Sydney cursed to bear a heavy sack of knowledge and solitude. At the upper end of St Jerome's playground, where it met a pedestrian crossing on Rossmore Avenue, there was a giant tree. For six years throughout primary school, I played under and around it. Its roots exploded through the tar beneath and its wisdom emerged from the ground like a lost tune. Its branches and leaves rose, sprawled and towered above like a cloud. Trapped and beautiful. Wild and safe. This tree had watched me grow. It had witnessed my loneliness and soothed my sadness. I went to the tree to cry, to tell it my secrets, to hide. One Lunar New Year as I walked past the tree, I saw a lucky red envelope sitting idly underneath it. There was no one around. I opened the small envelope and inside was twenty dollars! The tree smiled as I ran home to tell my mother.

So on my way home from the station, I crossed the road just to walk into the tree's soothing orbit. I was walking past the tree as I sensed the Jones sisters drawing closer.

Jessica asked her sister, 'What's the difference between ET and Asians?'

'I don't know,' Peta replied. 'Tell me.'

'ET got the message and went home.'

They laughed out loud then crossed over to the other side of the street. I was both humiliated and confused by this exchange. I *was* home. At least that's what I'd thought. Where else would I go?

Sticks and stones may break my bones but names will never hurt me. Sticks and stones may break my bones but names will never hurt me.

But what name had I been called exactly? And why did I feel so ashamed? I looked over at the tree. Its branches tried to reach out to caress me, having witnessed the exchange.

It was time for me to move schools. I was sick of ethnic wars. Sick of shame. I needed to soar.

A teacher at my school was switching to a new school down south called Bethany College. It had a junior campus in Kogarah and another campus at Hurstville for years nine to twelve. The uniform was maroon and grey. I decided to call the school to set up an interview with the principal. She was a lovely round lady with smiling eyes. When I showed her my school reports and grades she was baffled as to why I wanted to leave all my friends and go to Bethany, which wasn't close to where we lived. In hindsight, I don't understand how I was able to be brave enough to leave my school and friends. But I was too young to have developed a real sense of community—and far too focused. My sole objective was to succeed academically. My resolve came from a source far deeper than a uniform. A source I could only articulate when I slept next to my mother.

So I said goodbye to my MacKillop friends. It was bittersweet. A lot of the teachers and students thought that by my departure I was insinuating the school wasn't good enough for me. I know that they quietly resented my decision, given I was a star student.

At the time, my family had been vegetarian for about five years. A combination of Cao Đài scriptures, Buddhist teachings, Bible chapters and documentaries on Nostradamus about the end of the world had convinced my parents that we had a better chance of surviving Armageddon if we didn't eat meat. Animal meat would weigh down our spirits. Only a few years earlier, in primary school, my mother had made Văn and I eat steamed pigs' brains for intelligence. The brains weren't even mashed in with vegetables or stir-fried. They were just squiggly clumps of nutty creaminess, straight from a school science room and flavoured with chicken stock. On one of my last few days at MacKillop, I decided I deserved a meat pie. At lunchtime I lined up at the canteen and furtively bought a pie with sauce. I sat alone and scoffed it down, making sure no one saw me. All my friends knew I didn't eat meat. One of my friends, a Vietnamese girl, was also vegetarian for the same reasons. I chewed the pie so fast my mouth was almost burned. I quickly went to the bathroom to wash out any lingering smell of meat. Then I returned to my friends who, thankfully, didn't suspect a thing. I was already a sinner. With the taste of a meat pie and teary goodbyes behind me, I left Mackillop Girls High School.

CHAPTER 7

A mouth to eat with

When I joined Bethany College, I was the only student of Vietnamese origin in my grade. It was another all-girls Catholic school but most of the families were far more affluent than those back at MacKillop. I would walk to the bus station near Punchbowl train station and catch the bus to Hurstville station. Forty minutes later I would arrive and hop onto another bus which would drop me off at Bethany. A friend of mine from MacKillop had already left to go to Bethany not long before I arrived. I joined her group of friends, which consisted of Australian-born girls of Malaysian, Greek and Yugoslavian descent.

I was still a repressed, sensitive and timid girl. But by now I had hairy legs and acne as well as my Best & Less shoes, and my mother still sewed most of my clothes. I quickly realised that I was practically the only one in the whole school who did not have brand-name shoes. Sports day was a torment. I don't know what it was but some of the students would occasionally make snide comments to me. I felt like an outcast. I decided I needed a pair of Nikes. I read in my local paper that a new McDonald's was opening in Punchbowl and they were hiring. My father drove me to the interview. It went well. But at the end of it, the interviewer realised that I was three months under the minimum legal working age. I couldn't believe it. 'Come back in three months,' she told me. But I didn't have three months! My acne wasn't going to fade, electrolysis was too expensive and in three months' time I would be even more isolated and bullied. I had to find a place that didn't mind child labour and would pay cash. There was only one option: Uncle Thanh and his wife's bakery in Matraville.

I worked hard on weekends, sweeping the floors, slicing the bread, making pork rolls and packing sweet buns. When I'd finally made enough money for a pair of Nike Airwalks, my mother and Văn accompanied me to the Rebel Sports warehouse on the Hume Highway in Bankstown. The smell of fresh tennis gear, cotton and polyester gym pants, dry-fit shirts and new treadmills was intoxicating. New smelled oh so good! The aisles of shoes opened to me like a shrine of glorious Nike divinity. I glided down the aisles until I found them: white, green and a swoosh of pink. As I held them in my hands, I was overcome with pure joy. It was a religious experience. With my Nikes I would be reborn. I would be saved.

The next day was sports day. At school assembly, several girls in my class who had never spoken to me before commented on how cool my shoes were. The new untainted white glowed brightly beneath me. I hovered.

When I went back to McDonald's three months later, the store had already opened. I was interviewed by the store manager. Because I didn't have reports from Bethany yet I showed him my grades from MacKillop along with evidence of my extracurricular activities.

The manager looked at me and said earnestly, 'Mate, don't get a job here. Look at the potential you have. Go make something of yourself.'

I didn't get it. 'But I need a job.'

He got up and left. I sat there on the hard plastic chair bolted to the tiles. A fast-food flurry of customers, orders and uniforms golden-arches whirled around me. I was crushed.

Not long afterwards, I was walking through Bankstown Square after school one afternoon. Down the escalators from Target, the smell of baking cookies seduced me. Macaroons, Anzac biscuits, brandy snaps, white choc chips and harlequins beckoned from buckets, boxes and cellophane bags. The guy at the Cookie Man was Asian, maybe even Vietnamese. I decided to get a bag of mixed cookies and a job.

The owner had the same name as my younger brother. He was indeed Vietnamese. After a quick conversation, he told me I could start on Thursday. He offered me three shifts a week.

The mixed bag of cookies tasted great. I ran home to my mother to tell her the good news.

Once a week I worked with a lovely girl whose parents were from Macedonia. We took turns serving at the counter while the other packed the cookies. One day I short-changed an elderly man. He wore comically large sunglasses that clipped onto his reading glasses. 'I thought you Asians were supposed to be good at maths,' he snapped. 'This totally changes my whole belief.' I fumbled around in the register for the correct change, my back turned to him, my cheeks burning with humiliation. I wasn't a person. I was a race. *You Asians.* When he left, the girl I worked with tried to cheer me up by telling me a silly story. I don't remember the story. But I remember how hot my cheeks felt and how the smell of cookies suddenly didn't seem so nice anymore.

But not long after that incident, I remembered why I quite liked working at the cookie store. I got to have fleeting conversations with different people and every now and then something amusing would happen. On one occasion I served a woman with senior citizen pink hair and grand pearl earrings. I wasn't sure whether I short-changed her or not. I looked at her for some impending reprimand. I wasn't sure whether all her eyebrow hairs had moulted or whether she had deliberately shaved them like Whoopee Goldberg. She had pencil-drawn eyebrows but had forgotten to draw in the eyebrow on the left. It made her powdered face carry a constant look of surprised confusion, as though some surprise a few stores back made one of her eyebrows just pop out like a three-dimensional storybook. She put her change in her purse and left. I exhaled. Then I checked both my eyebrows. Just in case.

My poor mother didn't know what to do about my hairy legs or acne. She'd never encountered such first-world problems in Vietnam. She spent what she could spare of the government's child-assistance payments for low-income earners on waxes, creams, cleansers and facials. In the Priceline at Roselands shopping centre, I would read aloud from the packaging of different products, translating for my mother, who was a typical hairless Asian. When ballroom dance lessons began with the local Marist Brothers school, I hid behind a fringe that covered half my face and kept my gaze permanently fixed on the floor. I couldn't understand it when a Korean Australian boy, who was the cuter of twin brothers, said he liked me. At the bus stop outside Hurstville's Hungry Jack's, we sat as far apart as possible on a bench across from the blazing neon lights of the store. I was paralysed with awkwardness. I think I said my parents were really strict and I couldn't see a movie with him until I had finished university. (I honestly believed this. My mother did tell me once that I could only have a boyfriend once I graduated. From university.)

At school I continued to excel but was bullied by a girl who was a bit of a troublemaker. She could sing really well, though. The combination of hairy legs, acne, homemade clothes, discount-store shoes and a reputation as a studious geek made me an obvious target. The girl hung out with a group whose members also felt it was funny to stop me from leaving the classroom after I'd gathered my books. At the doorway, a freckled brunette girl with oily hair towered over me, her arm extended to block my exit. After a minute or so of asking her to let me through while she laughed scornfully, I just looked up at her and said, 'Fuck you. Let me through.' The girl was as shocked as I was. I clutched at my cheap contact-covered exercise books, unsure of where that expletive had come from. I had never sworn before that moment. Bewildered and silent, the girl let me pass. I walked out of the room, riddled with shock and guilt. I went to my religion teacher, who was also my year coordinator, and told him what had happened. I was looking for absolution because I had said the F-word. Struggling to conceal a grin, he said it was okay. I think he was secretly proud of me.

I participated in an after-school science project. We were to make a telescope and enter it into a competition at the University of New South Wales. Our small group worked on it for months. We experimented with various materials in order to grind the lens slowly enough to get a precise concave. The end result didn't look very nice, but it worked. One afternoon, we waited after school until nightfall, then took it in turns to look through our telescope made from a discarded industrial pipe during laborious hours in the lab. I saw the moon up close for the first time in my life. I saw Venus. I saw stars. I saw a world where ancestral spirits waltzed from one planet to the next, where my wishes to them were kept safe, where my daydreams would become night dreams and then particles of sunlight. Simply magic.

I started up a St Vincent de Paul district youth group at my school. I contacted hospitals and day centres for mentally disabled kids. I coordinated volunteers (mainly my group of friends) to visit in the school holidays. I participated in debating again. At sixteen, I decided to enter a public-speaking competition. I had grown more confident. The Rostrum Voice of Youth competition was a statewide affair with district and regional rounds. My teachers travelled with me to each competition. As a new school that was relatively unknown, they were proud to see me representing Bethany and beating students from selective high schools and prestigious private grammar schools. I made it all the way to the state finals, which were to be held at the National Maritime Museum at Darling Harbour. Students from around the state were to be put up at a hotel near Hyde Park for a couple of days. I had never stayed in a hotel before. My family and teachers were going to be at the finals. The pressure to win was immense. I wanted my parents to be proud of me.

A couple of days before the event, I was in the library after school. Everyone had gone home and the library was closing. My year coordinator, an amazing and compassionate man, sensed that I wasn't okay. He sat opposite me. At the time, I couldn't articulate that part of my mission was redemption. For my mother, for my father, for Hồng Khanh believed to be killed in the Cambodian jungle—for all those who hadn't made it. I mumbled something about the refugee life, about wanting to make my parents happy, about being helpless, about the absolute imperative to win. To win would be a visible victory; it would in some part make the endless sewing and factory shifts worth it. I sobbed into my hands.

My year coordinator sat there and listened to me, a sixteen-year-old child with droopy, heavy shoulders. Then he told me that my parents were already proud of me, something I did not believe. He took out his wallet, withdrew a card and handed it to me. It had been given to him several years ago by a special person, he said. 'I've been carrying this card with me for a long time. I was told to part with it when I met someone special. Someone who needed it. I want you to have it. When you meet someone special who needs it, you too will pass it on.'

I took the card. It was a simple piece of cardboard, a little curved from being pressed in the wallet. There was a small calendar on one side. On the other was printed: *I am and I can. With God's strength.* I would keep that card with me for about eight years until I passed it on in turn.

I sat there at the library desk, holding the card in my hand. I knew it wasn't enough. I knew that it would not give me the power to win the competition, to redeem all the pain and suffering of my family, to heal us. But I placed it in my wallet and thanked him.

The next day in school assembly, my year coordinator led the school in prayer. He made special mention of me and how proud the school was. He asked the school community to pray that I do my best. That was all that was asked of me. I bowed my head in an attempt to slide further down into my second-hand blazer as I felt hundreds of eyes on my back.

That weekend, my parents drove me to the city. We rarely ventured into town. The series of intimidating one-way streets and tall buildings disoriented us. My father got lost and drove around the same block several times until I just got off at a hotel that had the words *Hyde Park* on the front. I told my parents just to go home and assured them that I would be okay. My mother was in tears with worry. It was the wrong hotel, but I managed to find the right one.

There I met the other contenders. They had come from schools all across the state, including rural New South Wales. We were taken to Australia Square for lunch at the Summit, an expensive revolving restaurant on the forty-seventh floor. I felt out of my depth in such grand surrounds. I had never seen Sydney from this viewpoint. The city stretched out below us like a giant patched carpet. I was far from the safety of my working-class suburb. I wasn't meant to be there with students from schools that had tennis courts and sweeping acreage, students whose parents spoke fluent English and drove cars that didn't have cancerous rust around the wheels. I missed my family.

The night before the event, I couldn't sleep. Our group's leader was a pudgy man, probably in his late twenties or early thirties. Obviously sensing my discomfort, he tried to boost my confidence. He told me that I was smart and relatively attractive with a reasonable nose. I didn't understand why he specifically mentioned my nose. Immediately I leaped to the conclusion that there was in fact something wrong with my nose. His pep talk left me feeling worse about myself than ever.

It was my family's first visit to the National Maritime Museum at Darling Harbour. My father wore a suit. I saw my teachers in the audience. I saw in them their aspirations for my victory. The competitors nervously paced outside the auditorium. It was one of those theatres where the sound was completely contained and the lighting was dramatic. James, a student from Broken Hill with a blond mop, was really sweet. He tried to help calm my nerves. His charming crooked smile revealed two teeth that weren't flush with the rest. I loved his protruding teeth. They were perfectly imperfect.

We all had to deliver a prepared speech and an impromptu speech. The topic of the impromptu speech was given to us after the prepared speeches were presented. We had ten minutes to prepare and then it was my turn. They pronounced my name correctly; that was a good start. I walked onto the stage and the spotlight was so bright in my eyes that I couldn't see the audience. Everyone was swallowed by the darkness but my mother's face flashed at me from somewhere on the right. I wore my lucky velvet maroon clips on either side of my head, just above my ears. Standing up on the stage, it was clear to me that I wasn't good enough. The inadequacy I'd felt gazing at the view from the Summit seeped into the theatre. The stitches of my father's Hard Yakka uniform and the hum of the sewing machine crept into the theatre and perched themselves on seats in the front row. Drained of confidence, I gave a lacklustre performance.

When all the speeches were done, the competitors were invited on stage for the announcement of the results. I didn't win. I wasn't even runner-up. I forced a smile, but I was devastated. My teachers and family posed with me for photos. The loss of that day would haunt me for some time to come. There was nothing anyone could do to soothe me. The idea that I could be so close but not good enough embedded itself in me. I never participated in a public-speaking or debating competition again.

The only bright side of the whole debacle was that James and I became penpals. He wrote to me from Broken Hill and I responded. I looked forward to receiving his letters. There was nothing romantic about them; it was just an easy natural communication between two awkward teenagers who somehow knew they didn't belong.

One day I came home from school to find my parents in a rage. My father had opened my mail. He saw a male Anglo name at the end of the letter and was overcome with a fear whose seeds had been planted years before I was born. Back in Vietnam, secret lovers would write letters to each other with promises to elope. Also, my father had done his military service sometimes alongside white Americans. He knew that some of them had a hunger for women that resulted in the rapes of Southern Vietnamese villagers. In Vietnam, during the war every time an American came into the house, my mother and her sisters would hide underneath the wooden beds, praying that the lustful white man would not find them. They would hold their breath, eyeballs locking onto army boots, hands clasping hands.

My father couldn't even look at me while he yelled. He said I had to stop communicating with this boy immediately. If I ever married a white boy, he would disown me.

I demanded to know why they had opened my mail. They were baffled that I could even ask such a question. If they had given birth to me, they had the right to take my life. My right to personal space and privacy was nothing against all of their rights over me as parents. As people whose daily sacrifice for me involved the forgoing of dignity, of sleep and of home.

I stopped responding to James. His letters grew shorter, the intervals between them longer. Then they stopped. But my parents didn't open my mail again.

•

As I successfully navigated in-grown hairs and began taking dermatologist-prescribed medication, I became a little more comfortable at Bethany. One day in commerce class we were discussing where our parents worked. My father was still working as a machine operator at F. Muller. On forms my mother was either a housewife or a tailor. Neither seemed to articulate sweatshop worker or garment outworker appropriately, but we didn't want to embarrass the reader of the forms.

When I named the company my father worked for, a girl in the class said, 'My dad works there too! He's the general manager. Maybe they know each other. What does he do?'

I felt the familiar burn on my cheeks. 'He's a machine operator.' I doubted that the general manager knew my father.

He was just a nameless, faceless worker on the noisy factory floor.

'What's your dad's name? I'll ask Dad whether he knows him.' It was a naive request, one which could only have come from a teenager who knew nothing of forklifts and second-hand furniture. I dreamed of one day buying brand-new clothes. She lifted the hem of her tunic in the hallway to show her friends the tan she got from the family's trip to their holiday house. My father called her dad 'sir'. We were the daughters of employees at the extreme ends of the food chain, sitting together, learning about economics. The difference in our circumstances stung me.

Year ten was coming to an end. I decided to join the yearbook committee. Everyone was asked what they wanted to be when they grew up. They were also asked to provide a quote. Occupations ranged from lawyers to teachers to musicians. Quotes included the usual *Friends forever* and *Dance like no one is watching*. I said I wanted to be either a jockey or Peter Pan. I was small enough to be a jockey, and it was unlikely I would grow much more, given I took after my father's side of the family. I can't explain Peter Pan. My quote was my own: *Dare to be yourself. You can love me or hate me. But at least you will know me.* It was more of a self-help aspiration than a statement. Deep down, I knew I didn't dare to completely be myself.

Everyone was excited about the year ten formal. Who to bring? What to wear? How to do one's hair? I had no answers for any of these questions. In the playground, girls huddled together to plan the biggest event of their teenage life. Meetings would be held at various houses, presided over by glowing mothers proffering advice and hot chocolate. Tanning powder and horsehair brushes would be ordered from infomercials. Meanwhile, I begged my mother to allow me to go. It was to be held at Hurlstone Park RSL on Canterbury Road. Văn put in a good word for me. He had paved the way for me already by attending his own formal a couple of years earlier. In the end, it was decided that I could go as long as I had a chaperone. We settled on our neighbour, Văn's friend, who was eighteen at the time and could drive. Since my mother knew his mother it would be safe for me to go with him. He would take our 1979 Toyota Corona. The bubbles of rust bursting through the white paint. I managed to find a simple long black dress on sale. The girls in my school group had older dates who drove two-door sports cars.

After the event was over, the group decided to head to the city for an impromptu after-party. A combination of testosterone, ego and Punchbowl grit overwhelmed my date; he decided he could keep up with the shiny convertibles. He floored the Corona. I was stunned into silence. We accelerated well beyond the speed the car had ever been driven. Then a convertible sped up beside us. We looked over and saw the driver mouthing something and gesturing. My date ignored them, probably assuming that they were saying that the car wasn't bad for her age. He pressed harder on the accelerator. The convertible fell behind then sped up to us again and this time the driver was shouting. I looked around. There were sparks shooting from the exhaust. I yelled at my date to pull over.

We found a spot to stop but the car wouldn't start again. I was hysterical. It was my family's only vehicle. It was essential to our livelihood. While my date called for roadside assistance, I walked away to a shrub and crouched down, sobbing in my discounted dress, under an urban sky somewhere near Ashfield. Eventually the roadside patrol arrived. After inspecting the car, the mechanic told us that the engine had overheated and we just needed to wait for it to cool down. When at last the car started we drove home mostly in silence. It was way past my curfew. As I walked into the house, I realised I didn't have the luxury of being like my classmates, of doing what they did. That evening I had risked my family's only asset: an asset we depended on to take my father to work, to deliver the garments, to buy cheap groceries at Flemington markets. That evening, I was reminded of my place; of where I came from and the pleasures I couldn't afford.

MacKillop and St John's were also having their year ten formal. I had met a sweet boy from St John's during the debating season. When I was up against his team, he withdrew from that debate because he didn't want to debate me. He sketched a picture of Sydney Harbour for me and wrote out the words to Oasis' 'Wonderwall' on a piece of paper as a gift. When he asked me to be his date for his formal, my mother let me go because he was Vietnamese and Catholic. My date's dad would be driving us to the venue, and I decided to wait out the front of our house.

While I waited a congregation of beautifully dressed girls gathered on Karissa's porch. Karissa had stayed on at MacKillop and I rarely saw her after I changed schools. I watched, dumbstruck, as two stretch limousines with sunroofs pulled up out the front. Several good-looking guys emerged from the vehicles, carrying flowers. Karissa's mum and older sister were taking photos of them all, everyone beaming proudly and wafting around like a Chanel No. 5 scent.

I stood there on my porch in the same discounted black dress recycled from the last formal, clutching my Salvation Army purse. I turned to go back inside the house when I heard a beep. My date's dad waved from the driver's seat. I sighed with dread. My cheeks burned and throbbed. I wish I could have taken the blup-blup-blup inside my cheeks and thrown it at the bottom of the poinsettia tree in the corner of the front yard. With my head down and right hand holding up the length of my dress, I quickly moved towards the vehicle, hoping that my envy and I could slip by Karissa unnoticed into the car. In the backseat, my self-pity sat imposingly beside me.

•

With the Higher School Certificate two years away, I needed to maximise my chance of success. For this reason, and the fact that Catholic school fees and uniforms were forcing my mother to sew longer and longer hours under dim lights, I decided to compete for a spot at an academically selective high school. The fees would be much cheaper. The biggest intake after year seven was for year eleven. One weekend I went to St George Girls High School to sit an exam in maths and English. I did well enough to earn a spot. My teachers at Bethany were sad to see me leave. I knew that my spiritual needs were not going to be nurtured at this public school but the way that the Higher School Certificate worked meant that the marks I would get at an academically selective school would be moderated against students in the state, resulting in adjustments in my favour for my final grade to enter university.

One afternoon, just before dusk, I was at home studying when I heard the car pull into the driveway. I knew this meant my father was home. Usually he would take off his steel-capped boots in the garage and air out his thick socks before entering the house. But after some time had passed and he didn't come in, I went out to the garage. He was sitting on a milk crate. He used my old primary school bag as his work bag. My mother would pack a lunch of yesterday's dinner stacked inside round aluminium trays held together by a long handle that clicked in place. The bag, boots and lunch container were piled neatly around him. I looked at my father. He seemed different somehow. He was like some sort of withering creature born with a naturally sad face. He looked broken and defeated with the type of melancholy I previously heard from my uncles, which is so powerful it changes the lines on your palms.

I asked him what was wrong. He began to describe the abuse, the torment, the racism that he was subjected to at work and the placid face that he is forced to wear every day. On this particular day, a fellow worker decided to sabotage the multi-million-dollar machine my father was operating during his shift. This worker took a handful of tiny screws and threw them into the machine.

Production was stopped. Time costs money. Money costs jobs. Jobs were how you supported your family.

My father never told me what happened in the re-education camp, but I learned from my uncles that inmates were forced to denounce themselves repeatedly, chanting that they were traitors to their country. I imagined the hundreds of times my father would have been made to repeat these words. And now in Australia he was just another mute migrant. Anger, fear, resentment, pity, terror and sadness had rolled over him like waves. Finally, pushed beyond endurance, that day my father imploded. Like a crazed rabid animal he had grabbed a metal rod and headed towards the culprit to attack him. But before he could strike his target, reason took hold. What would happen to us if he went to jail? He dropped the rod along with the last remnants of his pride. My teenage heart was breaking into tiny bits of pulp as he recounted the story. Then he looked at me and said, 'In this country I have a mouth to eat with but I don't have a mouth to speak with. You are my voice.'

That day marked a turning point for me; I saw my future. There would be many others just like my father who needed a voice to speak for them. They needed access to justice and representation. And I realised that my father was the bravest man I knew. It took courage to walk away. It took resilience and discipline to wear a placid face no matter the hurt he was suffering inside.

Inside the house my mother had stopped sewing and was getting dinner ready. I had seen her cry silent tears. I had seen her lose everything she owned and start again without breathing a word of self-pity or complaint. As I looked at my mother, with bits of thread in her hair, holding the fish sauce bottle over the pot on the stove, I knew I was seeing the most graceful and compassionate woman I would ever know.

That day I vowed I would do whatever I could to be worthy of being my parents' daughter, a daughter of this family—a family that was surviving.

CHAPTER 8

Someone to lean on

I was a little more comfortable at St George Girls High School than I had been at my previous schools. It was an academically selective school and enrolment at the school had not been an easy task. I discovered it was acceptable to be ambitious and to be smart. And the uniform code was less rigid than the Catholic schools I had attended; I could wear it shorter. The day before school started, my mother hemmed my dress and asked me why it had to be so short. I told her that it was the standard at this new school. The truth was that I was still as slight as a child and my boobs didn't seem like they wanted to grow; a short dress was all I could do to look good.

One late afternoon not long after I started at St George Girls, I had stayed late at the library to do some research, so most of the students had gone. As I left and walked towards Kogarah train station alongside the fence of another school, I saw two girls from a local public high school come towards me. Many of the students from other high schools had a strong dislike for St George girls, who they believed acted as if they were smarter and better than everyone else. As the girls came nearer, they moved towards my right. I sensed something was going to happen but didn't react quickly enough. When they reached me, they rammed me against the steel fence, their bags heavy against my body. Then they just kept on walking. I turned around and yelled 'Bitch!', to which one of the girls yelled, 'What did you say to me?' and started coming towards me. Luckily the other girl pulled her back and they kept on walking. I was angry and confused. What had I done? Why did this have to happen to me? I walked as briskly as I could to the train station with my head down. My body burned with rage. I had to find a group that I could cling to.

The student body for each grade was much larger than I had expected. Most of the new girls who joined in year eleven were of Asian backgrounds. I met a couple of girls who, like me, had joined St George in year eleven and were Vietnamese. They also lived nearby in Bankstown. We caught the same train every morning and got off at Sydenham station to change for a train to Kogarah. From there it was a short walk to school. Naturally we merged into the existing large group of students of Chinese, Hong Kong and Malaysian origins. There was the odd girl of Indian or Anglo descent who latched on like Asian groupies. We didn't mind them. Our group of Asians mainly wore glasses, straight fringes, long hair and were huge fans of Hello Kitty. None of us went to dance parties. There were FFKs (Fresh from Korea), ABCs (Australian-Born Chinese) and FOBS (Fresh off the Boat). There were also girls of Asian origin who hung out with the Anglo 'skips'. They spoke with ocker accents. Some even skateboarded. There were lesbians who clustered together like a mixed bag of candy, proud to be misfits who challenged anything conventional.

In one of the first weeks of school, there was a study camp. I had not yet aligned myself with any group in particular, and was still getting to know my fellow students. So I visited the lesbian group in their bunks and had a chat. They were all very friendly until a tall girl with a pixie cut, obviously the unofficial leader of the group, entered the room. 'What is this?' she demanded. 'A tea party? Get out!' I immediately left the room. Over the next two years she would remain an intimidating presence. I never loitered around the year twelve study room, a special room with a kitchen and lounge reserved only for girls in their final year. This girl and her crew had made the room their domain. None of the Hello Kitty Asian girls hung around there. We were playground and library girls.

I never spoke to the pixie-cut lesbian until the last week of high school. Before school ended, some girls got together to hatch plans to trash our brother school, Sydney Technical High School. They painted a huge sign emblazoned with the word WANKERVILLE. A group of them were supposed to sneak into the boys' school to hang it up one evening. Apparently there were a lot of meetings to discuss how to best trash the school while they were there hanging up the sign.

By the time the end of year twelve came around I had become more confident. I had my provisional driver's licence and I was on the edge of entering the world beyond high school. I was brimming with a constant sense of anticipation but was also heavy with an escalating desire to prove myself. One night, I made cards with the word *Wankerville* written on them in thick blue texta. After everyone was asleep, I snuck out of the house with the keys to the Corona. I don't know how my parents slept through the thunderous ignition and unmistakable screech when I over-turned the key. I then drove to the boys school in Hurstville. I parked the car on a side street and my heart pounded in my chest. I slowly walked to the school and jumped over the fence. I had never been to the school before that night and didn't know the layout. After looking around for a while, I found the main playground. I took the cards from my bag and scattered them across the asphalt. In the bluish black of the night, the white cards glowed like brilliant patches of snow.

After my bag was emptied, I decided to run. The girls at school had talked about the security shifts at the boys school and the best times to get in and out but I hadn't paid attention. I bolted across the school towards the fence, climbed over and raced back to where I had parked the car. Sweat clung to my body. Each breath felt like a weighty sonic boom emitting from deep inside my lungs. My pulse raced with fear and adrenalin. Then from the shadows I heard urgent whispers.

'Who's that?'

'I don't know.'

'Fuck, I think that's Cat Thao. Hey, Cat Thao!'

I moved towards the shadows. There were three of them, one holding the large sign. I recognised Pixie Cut.

'Who are you with?' she asked.

'I'm not with anyone,' I replied.

'Are you serious? You came by yourself? What did you do?'

I told them about the cards, and then I left them in the shadows. That was the first conversation I had had with that girl since the camp. I don't think they ever did hang up that sign.

The next day, as we rehearsed the year twelve graduation ceremony in the assembly hall, news was spreading about my prank. I had a few girls come up to me and tell me how gutsy I was. Even Pixie Cut looked at me differently that day. I had never intended for anyone to find out. The whole thing was silly and didn't have any real purpose. But as I sat there in the hall, with the tune of the school song emanating from the piano, I felt proud of my immature burst of courage.

•

I had always been wilful and stubborn. My parents never forced me to study hard. I went the extra mile because I decided to do so. I had always resented instructions and detested direction. But during those last two years of high school, somehow these qualities coalesced into brazen ego. One lunchtime, one of my friends said that she bet I couldn't ride a bicycle from Punchbowl to Hurstville in less than a certain time. The distance was only about seven kilometres but it was the time limit that was the challenge. I have no idea how the subject had come up; I didn't even own a bicycle at the time. Nevertheless, I proclaimed that I could do it. I saved up the money to buy a red bicycle from Kmart and set out one Saturday to ride from Punchbowl to Hurstville. As I was speeding downhill on Bonds Road in Roselands, a magpie suddenly swooped at me, causing me to lose balance. I fell off my bike and skidded down the road, straight into the pole of a bus stop. My new bike had been flung into the middle of the road and my shins and knees were bleeding. But with my friend waiting for me at Hurstville, I had no choice but to get up and keep on going. I made it there in time. When I reported my success to my friends on Monday the adulation they expressed didn't give me the joy I had anticipated. I'm sure they gained a little insight into my personality, the insecurity masked by a facade of bravado and fearlessness.

Foolish dares aside, I still channelled every ounce of energy into study. This was the world that I could control. Six times a week I attended extra tutoring for maths, physics, chemistry and English. On weekends, I read the *Financial Review*, *Time* magazine and *The Economist*. One day, scanning *Time* magazine, I saw an article about Eddie Adams and the Vietnam War photo that won him the Pulitzer Prize. It was the image of South Vietnamese police chief General Nguyễn Ngọc Loan executing a Việt Cộng prisoner somewhere in Saigon on 1 February 1968. The general has his back turned to the camera. His arm is almost fully outstretched, holding a handgun to the head of the prisoner. The general wears a sobering look of unflinching resolve. His target is squinting obscurely in anticipation of the bullet. A soldier dressed in camouflage looks on, the shadow from his helmet concealing his eyes. From the black and white photo, it is unclear whether the ground is covered with shadows from nearby trees or whether the road is stained with blood. In an article he wrote for *Time*, Eddie Adams said that while the general had executed the suspect, he, Adams, had killed the general with his camera. For as long as the general survived, long after that fateful photograph was taken, hate, cynicism and resentment latched onto the general's reputation like an incurable virus. His family would also suffer.

After I read the *Time* article, I asked my father about the photo. My father explained that it was war. People died. That just before the execution, the captured Việt Cộng had himself slaughtered some Americans. My father believed that all the images that came from the war, the images that helped to consolidate anti-war activism in the US and around the world, were part of a Communist propaganda effort to ensure the withdrawal of US troops. As horrific colour images from the jungles of South-East Asia appeared on televisions in homes of American and Australian families, people took to the streets. Crescendos of anti-war sentiment transformed into thousands of signed petitions rolling into the corridors of political decision making, which would end up in parliament. All the while, lieutenants like my father and former army doctors like my doctor in Cabramatta watched in dismay as military assistance was phased out. South Vietnamese soldiers battled on without bullets in their guns. My father, my uncles and members of the Vietnamese community drip-fed me their side of the story. I absorbed these one-dimensional stories about the war that destroyed their villages, their livelihoods and robbed them of their rightful places within the nation of their elders.

Outraged by the political machinations that had sentenced my family to a difficult refugee life, I wrote a letter to the editor of *Time* magazine. In it I said that especially in times of war, often truth is not what is conveyed from within a frame or from what is reported. The truth, I argued, might be found in what was not said. What was not photographed. What was not reported. *Time* published my letter.

It further cemented in me the one-sided history lessons and connection to the stories retold and relived by the Vietnamese war veterans in Australia. On each anniversary of the fall of Saigon, buses would transport people from all across Australia to Canberra, where they would stage protests outside the Vietnamese embassy. The yellow-starred red flag of the Communists would be torched along with dummies of the current Vietnamese president. Men would bring out their medals and stand to attention, clutching the old Republican flag of South Vietnam, yellow with three red lines. The yellow represented our race; the three red lines represented the three main regions of Vietnam—North, Central and South. Under this flag, the three regions would be unified. The old anthem would be sung, led by a community leader. It was an uplifting war cry to rally soldiers, villagers and young people, and was taught in Saturday Vietnamese school, to young Buddhist groups in Bonnyrigg, to Vietnamese scouts in Bankstown, to Vietnamese Catholic youth clubs in Revesby. This anthem would be forgotten in Vietnam, unlearned and untaught to an entire generation with no recollection of the Vietnam War.

Vietnamese community leaders worked hard to hold onto their truths, their stories and their fight to free Vietnam from the Communists' continuing oppression. The war was not over for them. It had only taken a different form.

•

As my senior years rolled on and studies became exhausting, Pauline Hanson began to rise to prominence. A year earlier, on 10 September 1996, while I was still at Bethany, Pauline Hanson had delivered her maiden speech in parliament after winning the seat of Oxley in Queensland. I watched in awe as she spoke of the 'reverse racism' suffered by white Australians as a result of Aboriginal assistance, of how the nation's immigration policy had led to the imminent danger of Australia being swamped by Asians. I wondered, was I part of this looming sinister Asian invasion? As I watched parts of her speech on the news, her words ejected from her mouth, swirling around her in the Australian parliament before they pierced through the television screen, pricking my face and arms like the blast of a thousand icicles. I thought about my place in this Australia.

'Between 1984 and 1995, forty per cent of all migrants coming into this country were of Asian origin. They have their own culture and religion, form ghettos and do not assimilate. Of course, I will be called racist but, if I can invite whom I want into my home, then I should have the right to have a say in who comes into my country.'

My country. My country.

These two words chiselled fault lines across the nation. Lines that became boundaries separating those who could use the word 'my' from those who couldn't. Insiders and outsiders. Wanted and unwanted. Australians by birth, by citizenship and by colour. Us and Them. Even those Asians who were born in Australia had to earn their right to live in this land of great opportunity. If you were an Asian sports star, celebrity chef, designer or newsreader who didn't live in a ghetto, you were okay. I was none of these things. Nor were my parents with their fragmented survivor English. *Yes, sir. Discount. Tomorrow pay you.* It was the language of a silent working-class minority whose children were sometimes born with inexplicable hurt from another time. Another life.

Most of the major political parties criticised Pauline Hanson's policies, which advocated a return to economic protectionism via the reintroduction of tariffs and the abolition of multiculturalism. Her provocative maiden speech divided the nation, but the prime minister of the day, John Howard, refused to publicly denounce her policies. Disillusioned by this lack of critical and timely leadership, I wrote a letter to *Time* magazine condemning the prime minister for his silence. It too was published.

As support for Pauline Hanson and her One Nation party flourished, students around the nation rallied to protest. I found out that a student protest in Hyde Park had been organised. Students were to walk out of school at midday. I photocopied hundreds of leaflets and posted them on the walls of the toilet blocks at school.

On the morning of the protest, I stood at the top of the stairs of Punchbowl station, handing out the flyers to students. Some people insulted me, others wished me luck. Ever since primary school I had written my school absence notes and got my parents to sign them. When they were too busy, I forged their signatures, knowing that they trusted me to administer my own learning. I also wrote and signed most leave notes for Vinh. That day, I wrote a note excusing myself from maths class and the rest of the subjects I had that day. At exactly midday, I rose from my seat. My teacher, who knew what was going on, said all she wanted was for me to be careful. I had persuaded a handful of girls to come with me. We had made protest posters. We caught the train to the city and got off at Town Hall, where students were starting to congregate. There was a festive atmosphere. Looking around, it was heartening to see such solidarity from fellow young Australians of all races, colours and creeds. Their eyes all echoed the desperate words of '*my country too*'. There were riot police and horses on George Street. As we began to march, whistles, drums and chants accompanied our progress, the sound spiralling outwards and upwards, along with our hopes for a true sense of belonging. *It is my country too.*

There were more protests as a crescendo of support for One Nation rose from farms, suburban streets and parliament. Before, during and after the rise of Hansonism, friends of mine of Chinese descent, whose family had been in Australia for five generations, were still greeted with exclamations of: 'You speak English so well!' The concept of what it meant to be Australian was still so rooted in the legacy of the White Australia Policy. As an Asian teenage girl growing up in Australia, decades after the policy was officially dismantled, a swirling sense of isolation and a lack of belonging began to engulf me. The ripples of One Nation developed in me a deep resentment of the white middle-class Australians who were the decision-makers, stars on popular soap operas, High Court judges, policy-makers and celebrity gardeners. I realised with horror that I had inherited my father's mouth: a mouth to eat with, not a mouth to speak with. No matter how much I protested or studied, my screams of rage played back in slow motion to an insignificant audience. A testimony blunted and unheard.

The growing negative perception of Asian Australians, particularly Vietnamese, was further compounded by the troubles in Western Sydney. I was fourteen when Cabramatta MP John Newman was murdered. Vietnamese-born Phương Ngô, a Fairfield local councillor, was convicted of orchestrating the murder. His appeal attempts were unsuccessful. The Vietnamese community had their own theories. Later, street workers, who had witnessed the sudden influx of drugs and the changes that would tear through the community, chatted to me about what was not reported, what was not investigated. About the subtext that only a handful of people who walked the cold streets knew. Cabramatta became known as the Vietnamese ghetto and the drug capital of Sydney. As young boys who had been placed on boats of escaping refugees grew up alone in Sydney, they banded together in a street family. In the nineties, it was said that we Vietnamese kids either became overachievers, gangsters or drug pushers. Kids from my part of Sydney lied about their address on job applications in the hope of avoiding the stifling stereotypes. In our own way, in the face of racism, sinister stereotypes and economic disadvantage as well as the usual growing pains of adolescence, we did what we could to just hold on. I was increasingly beset by feelings of confusion, hosting a dormant squalor of anger and pain. But the effort required to keep trying, to hold on, was wearing me down. I could barely fathom the prospect of a bright future. By the beginning of 1998, my Higher School Certificate year, I already felt weary.

We had moved again. We were still in Punchbowl, but this time on the other side of the railway tracks. Our landlords were actually our neighbours at Rossmore Avenue, who had purchased an investment property. The day we moved in, my mother dreamed about the spirits of the house. She saw a vicious murder of Aboriginal people taking place. The pain and the cries, still fresh, clung to the frame of the house. The spirits, torn into sharp shreds of bitterness, mourned in the roof, in the windows, in the floor. The rent was cheaper there and it was all we could afford. Because we knew the landlords we hoped that they would be kind to us. We had to stay. But my mother knew that the house was cursed. During our short time in that dim house, a series of mishaps occurred. My mother fell down some steps and was on crutches for months. Sewing was excruciating. My father became sick. After almost fifteen years of working as a machine operator, he was forced to stop work. Vinh's asthma flared up and I grew ever more tired.

The Higher School Certificate was a blur. I didn't go on the year twelve boat cruise or to any of the major school parties. Occasionally I caught a train to the city on Thursday afternoons when we got off early for sport. I would go to Galaxy at Town Hall on George Street, the arcade games capital. I would play Street Fighter and Tekken. My favourite Tekken character was King, a Mexican luchador who cared for nothing except fighting. In fights he wore a leopard mask that made him look like a mythical lord. Later, having faced death, he was rescued by priests. In repentance he decided to build an orphanage. He enters the King of Iron Fist Tournament to win enough funds to build the orphanage. King had a wicked assembly of hybrid wrestling and martial arts moves. As I bashed on the buttons of the Tekken arcade game, I fell into the world of the screen, wrestling and kicking my way past school bullies to a charmed life.

Other than these few trips to the city, my final year of high school was a haze of late nights, Sally Morgan's *My Place*, mathematical induction, economic history, carbon compounds and physics equations. Occasionally I woke up drenched with sweat born of fear and anxiety, believing that I had missed the English exam. I was driven by a fierce need to succeed; success in the Higher School Certificate was a way for me to garner pride and respect for my family among both other Vietnamese families and Australian society at large. The end result was meant to be the redeeming saviour that would rid me of my demons.

I tackled assignments and exams with ferocity. My grades had been stellar since year 11. I came first in economics and maths. For the trial examinations in year twelve, I came first in English. But then it was time for the real exams. As sixty thousand students in New South Wales prepared to sit the exams, I suffered from a deep fatigue that imbued my whole being. After years of relentless effort, bolstered by rigorous study routines and spurred on by self-imposed impossible expectations, I had had enough. I had arrived at a peak and knew that the plateau had come. My energy had slowly been depleting, scattered in bits on the Bankstown line trains, buses and footpaths that had led me to the various schools and tutoring centres I had attended, every day. A strange apathy had taken over, and as I walked out of my last exam, I felt nothing.

Time went by between my last exam and the results. As I spent the days watching *Home and Away* and poring over junk mail, my apathy thawed and gave way to nervous, brittle anticipation for my results. My first university preference was to study a combined Bachelor of Social Work and Bachelor of Laws at the University of New South Wales. It was the only university in Australia at the time that offered this combined degree. It required a score of at least 99 out of 100.

The day the results were due, I couldn't breathe. My nerves twisted in my stomach and inside the chambers of my heart. I felt the heaviness of my parents' thousands of footsteps through Cambodia. At times they probably felt their feet were still wet from the ground of terrorising jungles and accidental blood.

My mother decided it would be good for me to go for a swim. We drove the ten minutes to Roselands swimming pool and my mother pretended to swim while I floated on my back, with children's playful screams echoing in my ears. I closed my eyes. The rays of the sun kissed my eyelids as I tried to breathe out the long-fermenting bubbles of pressure. My mother was calm as always. As she paddled closer to me, she gave me a look that said there was nothing more I could do; that it was up to fate now. Fate. Together with guilt and mysticism, this was the surrogate mother that raised me.

A couple of years earlier, Văn had completed his Higher School Certificate. My family trembled with happiness and Văn's cheeks were wet with tears of joy as he peeled open the envelope to learn he had got into the course of his choice. All I wanted was the same.

Unable to wait for the postman, I drove alone to the sorting centre at Lakemba to see if my letter was en route. It was still there. I picked up the envelope marked with the New South Wales Board of Studies logo on the outside. As I drove home, I looked at the envelope sitting beside me on the passenger seat. I silently chanted, 'Ninety-nine, ninety-nine, ninety-nine,' until the numbers rolled like the streaming rhythmic sound of a Disney cartoon train. When I got home, I retreated to my room, too tense to open the envelope in front of my parents. The cork-like linoleum floor and grey walls held their breath. The blinds shuddered. The Aboriginal spirits stopped wailing.

I fumbled through the various information sheets and raw score marks until I found the Universities Admissions Index. I read it three times: 98.95. There must have been a mistake. I quickly called the Universities Admissions Centre to see whether there was an error. No error. I called the Board of Studies. I later called the University of New South Wales after the selection for places had occurred to see whether I could somehow get in. There was no hope unless I repeated year twelve or chose another course and transferred into my preferred program a year later.

I lay on my bed that day and sobbed. I don't know how long I stayed there. The sun went down. The traffic on Punchbowl Road subsided then grew loud again. I heard countless series of pedestrian light beeps go from quarter note beeps to rapid fire beeps as some random person crossed the road just outside our house at the intersection. The neighbouring boys from down the road had come back with a stolen stash of bike parts and I heard them speaking. The air grew thick. I could smell a stir-fry from the kitchen. My parents' attempts to comfort me were futile. I was a failure. I had come so close. I didn't want second best. Second never mattered. Second meant my father asking blandly, 'Why didn't you come first?' There was no rage, no yelling, just a simple and dull question which somehow stung so much more than if it had been meant to hurt.

•

I was accepted into my second course preference, a combined Bachelor of Commerce and Bachelor of Laws at the University of Sydney, the oldest university in Australia. The course wasn't due to start for three months. It was a bizarre, vacuous experience, not having anything to study for. For as long as I could remember, school work had defined me. Achievements that I could attain within my domain of control were recorded in black text on report cards and in academic competition results. These successes were tangible, unequivocal. These scores didn't care about my postcode or my parents' income or the language I prayed in. Without an exam to study for and weighed down by deep disappointment, in those three months of dubious transition I drifted.

I began to hang around with a bunch of Asian boys from Sydney Technical College. I was a tomboy and the token girl in the group. Always clad in cargo pants and a loose T-shirt, I was just another one of the guys. Overnight, I morphed from a disciplined, studious, pious daughter to a joyriding delinquent who sometimes didn't even come home. I would take the car and disappear, driving around aimlessly until the early hours of the morning. My parents were appalled and astounded at my new behaviour. When my parents took my keys away, I snuck out of the house in the middle of the night anyway.

We did stupid things that boys do. We had midnight barbecues in the middle of a soccer field, eating carcinogenic sausages in the pitch black. We drove to the city and hung out underneath the harbour bridge, talking about nothing while the boys drank beer. We squeezed into one guy's family's Toyota Camry and drove around roundabouts with the handbrake pulled up, burning rubber, laughing hysterically. We switched petrol station numbers and stole ice-cream signs. The perpetual pressure of academic success had abruptly evaporated. I was lost in a new universe of liberty without any assignment or exam to act as my compass. But I delighted in this rebellion. For the first time, it felt like it was I who mattered and not my grades.

One evening, as we were removing the petrol station numbers in a suburban street in the inner-western suburb of Dulwich Hill, a neighbour called the police. When we saw the cops, we all split up and bolted in different directions like hunted foxes. I ran into a random driveway and hid behind a car. The police walked through the streets looking for us with torches. With my heart thumping, I cowered in the shadows while the torch light raked the front of the house, like a menacing lighthouse beam. I wondered what I would say to the house's occupants if they opened the door. Thoughts raced feverishly through my head. I was sweating. I felt my chest dampen and liquid beads accumulate on my eyebrows as I held my breath. When the cops finally moved on, I sat down in the driveway, pulse still racing. After a long while, I crept out of the driveway and headed slowly back to where I had parked the car. Everyone had scattered and the boys were nowhere to be seen. I paced down the cold, still street occasionally accented by white cones of streetlight. I reflected on what had happened. What if I had been caught? How could I do that to my family? It was an unwieldy reminder that I was not entitled to be a silly carefree young person. I recalled the night of my year ten formal and the sparks coming out of my family's only car. I finally got to the car and started to drive home. I remembered I could not afford to make mistakes.

I decided I should get a job. I looked in the community newspaper for administrative positions. It took me to a messy office situated within a bizarre junkyard. I had no clerical experience. I had only ever sold pork rolls and cookies. The young woman who had placed the ad was barely older than me; I presumed this was her family's business. Needless to say, it was obvious I was just looking for a temporary job and was not passionate about working in a junkyard. I floated through a variety of odd jobs, from telesales of roller shutters to stuffing junk mail into envelopes in a factory. I looked in the paper again. Pizza Hut always seemed to be looking for drivers, I noticed.

With the family's only car, I started work at a Pizza Hut just outside Lakemba in Western Sydney. I was the only female delivery driver in several districts. On the first day, I watched a three-hour induction video introducing me to Tricon, the corporation that owned Pizza Hut, KFC and Taco Bell. I learned about hygiene from mock accidents and comical re-creations. The video was embarrassingly dated, with 1980s hairstyles and over-scripted dialogue made worse by horrendous acting. After I endured the video in the back room, I emerged into the busy kitchen and was given a turquoise cap and collared T-shirt. It was too soon for me to get my own name tag, so I was given the name tag of a previous employee, Mohammed. On top of the minimum wage, I would get $1.86 for each pizza I delivered. The drivers lined up to be given their pizzas and dockets. On the way out, we each grabbed the promotional extras if customers had ordered a special deal. It could be a frozen cheesecake or a box of biscuit ice-creams.

One evening, I grabbed a couple of dockets and pizzas as usual, then looked at the address and momentarily froze. It was a street in Lakemba that a friend of mine lived on. All the major insurance providers refused to insure anyone living on that street. Even brokers were apprehensive. Statistically, it was the most robbed street in Sydney at that time. I opened the passenger door to the car and put the pizzas on the seat. I had been to my friend's apartment before on that street but only during daylight. As I cruised down the street looking for the address on the docket, I talked aloud to myself. The tabloid current affair shows on television sensationalised statistics and postcodes, I said, but I was a kid born of these streets. There wasn't anything for me to worry about.

When I finally found the apartment block, I parked the Toyota Corona and placed the heavy club lock across the steering wheel. The beloved Corona was a piece of reliable junk but it was an easy target. I went around the building to the side entrance and walked up the stairs to look for apartment number seven. The stairwell light was broken. As I ascended further and further up the stairs, the darkness swallowed me. It was completely pitch-black. The hot pizzas inside the insulated covers became heavy. I could hear nothing and see nothing. I put one of my hands in front of my face. I couldn't see it. I walked towards what I knew would be a door and slowly felt it for a number. I traced my fingertips across a cold metallic curve. The air was humid and cavernous. I felt the sheets of carpet melt beneath me like quicksand. It was apartment six. One more flight. I inched along, wary of falling.

Finally I found apartment seven and knocked on the door. I could feel the beat in my carotid artery knocking like a giant kernel against the lining of my throat. 'Pizza Hut! Delivery!' I stepped back. The door opened. Inside was a group of six or so men, huddled on and around a lounge. There was a strong smoky smell. They all had their shirts off. I bent my head down, hiding underneath my cap. The guy who'd opened the door went to get some cash. The men all looked at me and said something I couldn't understand. The man who gave me the money said, 'Keep the change,' and smirked like a cartoon villain. I didn't even bother counting the money. Later I found out the tip was fifteen cents.

I quickly left the building and prayed to my grandmother that my car was still there. *Please, please, please.* I wouldn't be able to face my parents if the car was gone. As I ran out to the street, she gleamed at me under the streetlight. A flood of relief washed over me. I looked at the Corona affectionately. The familiar bubbles of rust under the paint and broken metal trim were suddenly reassuring. I got in the car and opened the club lock around the steering wheel. I had parked the car in a small laneway. It was too narrow to do a full U-turn or even a three-point turn. I inched forward and back in what turned out to be a six-point turn. Without any power steering, it was a real effort. My forearms started to ache and I was sweating.

Finally I got out of the laneway and drove back to the store. The delivery had taken longer than the promised thirty minutes, the hallmark of Pizza Hut. The manager said, 'That took a while. Hey, you have a bit of chow mein on your face.' Chow mein? It was a while before I understood what he was implying, that I made some sort of detour, maybe even home to eat some food. A protest of some kind formed on my lips but wouldn't come out. All I could think was that chow mein was a Chinese dish, one that I hated. I was Vietnamese. Clearly we Asians were all the same to him.

'Next order's waiting for you. Hurry up.' I tried to spit out a seething insult but it never reached him. My cheeks burned.

I walked outside onto the busy street, desperate to get away from the wafts of baking dough and melting cheese.

Tarek, an Iranian American guy on a working holiday, said, 'You shoulda told 'im to fuck off.'

I retorted, 'And lose the chance to wear this uniform? No way.'

He laughed and got into his rented car.

The last time I wore the Pizza Hut uniform was at an eight-eenth birthday party. A girl from school invited me and I had to come straight from a shift. I grabbed an empty pizza box and scribbled *Happy Birthday* on the inside. When I arrived at the door in my uniform, my friend's mother really did think someone had ordered pizza. I'm sure she was offended as there was plenty of homemade Indian food. I went out the back to where the birthday girl was and said, 'Someone call for a delivery?' just like the red-headed Dougie in the Pizza Hut ads. My friend liked my hand-delivered pizza birthday message, despite the stench of pepperoni.

•

The boys I used to hang out with had gone to Queensland for a holiday. When they came back most of them got girlfriends. By this time I had started working odd jobs and was too tired to see them anymore, especially when I was still delivering pizza at night. In between their girlfriend time and my need to earn some money, we drifted apart.

Towards the end of the three-month break before university started, I became involved with the Vietnamese Catholic Youth Organisation. Needless to say, my parents were relieved. Văn was already a member of the group. There were retreats, camps and meetings. At each large communal gathering of Vietnamese Catholics, which often brought together over ten thousand people, the members of the youth group would be stationed at key points of Paul Keating Park in Bankstown, selling candles for the church. The yellow and red-striped flag of old South Vietnam flew high. We prayed for political prisoners in Vietnam who fought for religious freedom. We prayed for all those souls who did not make the journey to Australia like us, hoping that their deaths weren't in vain and one day Vietnam would become a democracy. Amen. When the Lunar New Year Tết festival came about, the Vietnamese community organised a three-day celebration at Warwick Farm racecourse. Stalls would be set up with Vietnamese bingo, grilled pork and barbecued corn, and a stage would feature Vietnamese boy bands and fashion parades. Depending on whether there was an upcoming election, the opening ceremony would attract the state premier, the opposition leader and sometimes the federal Minister for Citizenship and Multicultural Affairs. Sponsorship money poured in from community and business leaders.

Around the perimeter of the park, marquees were erected from poles and industrial sheeting, each housing fake *Ochna integerrima* trees with lifelike yellow blossoms, the kind that only flowered during Tết in Vietnam. Lucky red pockets were hung from their branches. Kids paid $1 for a lucky dip, hoping the pocket they chose would give them a greater return. As evening fell, lines of firecrackers were lit, sending up flakes of red paper that came down like a magical curtain. Vietnamese martial arts schools had crews of lion dancers who performed amid the exploding firecrackers, dancing like fearless warriors born again from ancient times.

The festivities at Warwick Farm were the community's attempts to preserve and celebrate sacred traditions. Despite having travelled for thousands of kilometres across treacherous seas and facing all manner of challenges in a new nation, home had come with them. For those three days in the middle of an Australian summer, on a racecourse near the Hume Highway, opposite a giant car dealership, Vietnam came to us.

Each year at the opening ceremony of the festival, academic awards were given out to students who had excelled in the Higher School Certificate. In the year I graduated from high school, the Vietnamese Catholic Youth Organisation had a food stall. I volunteered at the stall, taking orders and preparing the food. That year, I was to receive an award because I came fourth in New South Wales for English out of tens of thousands of students. I didn't think it deserved public merit but by the community's standards, it was good enough. There was a girl who got a perfect score of 100 for the Higher School Certificate. She was also pretty, nice *and* skinny. But I was sure she wasn't funny. Awards were given to a set of twins who'd scored something like 99.99 and 99.95. They wore their school jerseys on stage, their scores printed on the back. Seriously.

On the day of the ceremony I stuffed a traditional Vietnamese dress into my bag, intending to put it on just before I went on stage to receive my award. The food stall was incredibly busy. I was on my feet all afternoon and didn't realise that the ceremony had started until one of the other volunteers heard the announcements being made. I quickly got changed out the back of the stall and looked down at my feet. I was in sports shoes. I had forgotten to pack high heels to go with the dress! Frantic, the volunteers all checked their shoes to see whether I could fit into someone's decent-looking sandals or high heels. We walked up and down the aisles to see if there was a customer who would lend me appropriate shoes for five minutes. Finally we found something that would work. I quickly bolted across the dusty course, past miniature rollercoaster rides and through plumes of grilled-pork smoke to the back of the stage. I slipped on the shoes and got onto the stage. I was panting, my armpits stained with sweat, while my hair reeked of corn and shallots. The bottom of my white silk pants underneath the traditional *áo dài* had a visible rim of dirt. On the stage, the lights were bright. The MC spoke of the pride of the Vietnamese community residing in these young shiny hopeful stars. Our Future. One by one, the stars would collect their awards. I couldn't see my parents in the audience but I knew that they were there. I hoped that my father would be happy. I might not have come first, but it was recognition within the community that mattered. A community that spoke his tongue and understood about afternoon and night shifts, steel-capped boots, grease and deadlines. A community that knew my result was a marvellous achievement. I was handed a certificate and a piece of 18-carat gold donated by a Vietnamese jewellery store in Bankstown. The Vietnamese know that recognition is great, but gold is even greater. When the ceremony was over, I ran back down to the stall and got changed. I gave my parents the gold and was greeted with smiles and pats by the members of the youth group. The older women who cooked at the back laughed as I put on my sports shoes and returned the high heels to their owner. Exhausted, I went home that evening, award in one hand and my traditional dress in the other.

•

Just before university started, the tutoring college I had attended held an end-of-year function. I was the master of ceremonies. It was the first time many of my peers had seen me in a dress. Even to my own year twelve formal I had worn a red satin suit cheaply tailored by a Vietnamese woman who lived in Punchbowl. The tutoring college function was held at the Unicorn Restaurant above a Lebanese café in Bankstown, opposite the railway tracks. It was there that I met David, a tutor at the college. One of the games we played on the evening was a joke competition. He got on stage and told a disturbingly crude joke that he, at least, found devastatingly hilarious. He laughed profusely at his own joke while awkward groans could be heard in the room amid uncomfortable token smiles. I thought he was either brave or stupid. Since no one else participated in the competition, he won by default. David had a certain self-assurance about him and was quite solidly built for a Vietnamese guy. He was handsome and had an attractive no-nonsense Western Sydney streak. I concluded he was brave.

When David and I spoke at the event, he said he was only a year older than me. I didn't believe him—he seemed much older—so he took out his driver's licence to prove it. Maybe his inherent resilience and outward confidence was groomed from time at his high school, where occasionally police sniffer dogs patrolled the school grounds. Maybe it came of being the only boy in a Vietnamese family. From wherever it had derived, it was exponentially greater than my own, and I found it very attractive.

I waited for him to call me, but when two weeks passed without any communication, I decided to initiate contact. I got his number from the college and dialled.

'Hello? Is that David? Do you know who this is?'

'Yes. Yes, I do.'

'Do you want to meet up some time?'

'Okay. I'll be there in fifteen minutes.'

'Don't you need to know where I live?'

Apparently he was also a bundle of paradoxes. He did martial arts and protected his friends in street fights, but was too shy to call a girl. We began dating. At eighteen years old I held hands with a boy, kissed and drank alcohol for the first time. As the world rapidly opened up to me under David's loving and protective watch, I felt like a child in an expanding and infinite universe, full of delicious new experiences which whizzed around and through me like dancing dandelions.

My parents had no idea I was dating David. Around this time, we had moved from Punchbowl to Chester Hill, eleven kilometres northwest. The curse of the house we had been living in had begun to poison our minds and infect our sleep. Before the move to Chester Hill, I scanned the Vietnamese community newspapers for rentals and conducted my own inspections before providing a final list of recommendations to my parents. I found a place one street away from David's house. It was a clean, decent place with a granny flat where the landlords lived. My parents accepted my recommendation and we moved in.

Shortly after the move, I introduced them to David. We were both very nervous. He had a shaven head so when he prepared for the meeting he wore a beret as well as a collared shirt and sleeveless vest over the top. It took him seven minutes to walk over from his house. When he came to the door, my father took one look at him, said hello, turned around, grinned broadly and then vanished into the backyard. I was gleeful. Silent withdrawal was usually my father's tacit approval. (But sometimes, confusingly, this move also signalled tacit disapproval.) My mother chatted to David politely, asking about his family, when they'd arrived in Australia and what he was studying at the University of New South Wales. His parents both had white-collar jobs. His mother worked for a state government department and his father was an engineer. I found it baffling that they did not sew and work in a factory like most of the Vietnamese parents I knew.

My parents knew and approved of David's circle of friends—all Vietnamese guys from Cabramatta, Chester Hill and neighbouring Sefton. Even if they weren't all at university, they were temple-going boys who followed Vietnamese traditions disciplined by concepts of karma and honour.

David's house was another version of Karissa's. The interior decoration had catalogue-worthy items like fashionable furry rugs, gold-framed mirrors, bundles of cinnamon sticks and a jacuzzi. David and his dad had extended their house, undertaking most of the renovations themselves. David was a handyman and a natural protector. For the time we were together, I was grateful to be able to defer many practical challenges and decisions to him while maintaining a facade of invincibility to my parents. For the first time in my young adult life, I felt I had someone to lean on. Someone to cradle and rescue me. The lingering feelings of being out of my depth, inadequate and alone had subsided somewhat under his watch. To me, David was a working-class Vietnamese-born knight heading a Western Sydney cavalry.

But in the first few months David and I dated, I felt pangs of envy and self-pity each time I entered his home. The leather couch, the wall of family memories, children's drawings pressed onto plates, crystal glasses and bath salts and the softness of a stable crib pranced in front of me like a character in a musical. The raging pangs became less delirious over time, but provoked in me an aching desire to reward and heal my family with material pleasures. A house. A home. Comfort. Certainty. Security. But I was a soon-to-be university student with a government Centrelink Youth Allowance and irregular income from a series of odd jobs. Later, I set up a small floristry operation from home. Despite this, there was no way I could immediately provide for my family. I was haunted by the hardships suffered by my parents, who wouldn't hustle and cheat like others yet were constantly pounded by misfortune. All I could do was offer moments of gladness and specks of hope.

In 1999, a film called *Three Seasons* was showing at a cinema in Fairfield, about a fifteen-minute drive from Chester Hill. An American film made in Vietnam, it was about the poetry as well as underbelly of Ho Chi Minh City. It was Father's Day and I did not have a cent to my name. In the nineteen years since my family had arrived in Australia, my parents had never once set foot inside a movie theatre. In Vietnam, my mother had seen only one film on the big screen. I was determined to take advantage of this rare opportunity to take my family to see a Vietnamese-language film at a cinema in Sydney. I researched a few pawnbrokers in Bankstown until I found one that offered a decent interest rate, then I pawned my Nokia mobile phone. With the money, I took everyone out to the movies. It was my gift to them.

As I sat there in the dark, I looked over at my father and my mother and saw expressions of rare pleasure on their faces. Scenes of old and new Saigon swept across the screen in gigantic form. There was the familiar roundabout at Ben Thanh market, surrounded by cyclos and conical hats. The cinema was filled with the sound of Saigon banter and Vietnamese song. We saw the places we had passed when we toured the city by cyclo, me a child of eleven on my mother's lap. I knew that with the financial hardship we were enduring, my parents might never be able to visit Vietnam again. For nearly two hours, overdue electricity bills, stomach ulcers, misunderstandings and fiendish sewing contractors receded through the cinema doors and waited outside like a loyal pet. As the changing scenes flickered on our faces, in the safety of the dark, I quietly cried.

•

As my three months of freedom drew to an end, I made the most of being with David and his friends. They were a mix of struggling students who drank cases of beer on the university lawn, vocational and community college students, former prisoners and factory workers. They were men who struggled like many other men—with money, with love, with family, with dreams. They would often assemble in the backyards of some Western Sydney suburban house, grilling meat, singing karaoke, dissecting current affairs and hatching plans for a better life. Sometimes there would be huge marijuana plants lined up against the back fence. Although most of them had grown up in Australia, a deep sense of Vietnamese identity burned within them. As they drank VB beer, they would claim that it stood for Vượt Biên (the Vietnamese phrase commonly understood as the refugee exodus), Vì Bạn (for my friends) or Vợ Bỏ (abandonment by wives). With their depository of survival scars, they each had a profound understanding of loyalty, honour and pride. And I grew to love them all.

CHAPTER 9

Lush green lawns

Sydney University was a different planet. Every corner of aged sandstone and manicured lawn was unfamiliar to me. I could never have conjured up such a setting even in my dreams. In those early months of university I felt intimidated and out of place. In my first law tutorial, which had about twenty or so students, I quickly discovered that most of my peers came from privileged backgrounds. They had an unabashed interest in money. Only two students in the class declared that they had chosen to study law because of social justice. One of those two students was me. When we discussed ways to diversify court benches, I advocated affirmative action to diversify the student body, ultimately diversifying the composition of lawyers and judges. One student argued that this was problematic because people from Western Sydney didn't aspire to be lawyers but instead wanted to become mechanics. Surely we shouldn't coerce people into doing something they didn't want to do. The shallowness and utmost lack of insight of comments like this repulsed me. It poisoned my view of a peer group that I was condemned to associate with for the next five years.

I welcomed the diversity of the commerce faculty, by contrast, comprising international students as well as students from all parts of Sydney, some of whom were aspiring entrepreneurs. I blended in with Islamic, Chinese and Iranian students. Still, I could not find a sense of community within the lush cricket grounds, the Old Teachers College or the lunchtime banter in the Wentworth Building canteen. Although I had earned a place at the oldest and most prestigious law school in Australia, I felt it wasn't my birthright – that I was and always would be a visitor. I hadn't wanted to go to this university anyway.

I turned in my first law paper, and it was returned to me with a request that I see the tutor. I had barely passed. Apparently my English was incredibly poor and my tutor recommended I seek help from the Intensive English Language Centre. I hadn't had my English criticised like that since year two when I was eight years old. I was disappointed and confused. That day, paper in hand, I walked towards Redfern train station, the nearest stop to the university. As usual, I handed a muesli bar to a beggar outside the station and rode the Bankstown line home. The same houses, backyards, graffiti that I would see thousands of times whizzed past me as I fell into a reflective trance. My mother and I had seen my name in the *Sydney Morning Herald* under the

English scores only a few months earlier. I had come first in the Higher School Certificate Trial Exams for 2 Unit English at an academically selective school. Lines from *Macbeth*, Sally Morgan's *My Place*, Peter Goldsworthy's *Maestro* crowded my brain and flooded me. I recalled memorised analysis of poetic devices used by the poet Bruce Dawe. Signs continued to stream past and words buzzed inside me. Belmore. Lakemba. Rhyming couplets. Wiley Park. Punchbowl. Iambic pentameter. Bankstown.

●

I'd enrolled at Sydney University with a friend called Peter who was studying for the same degree. Peter had attended the same tutoring college as I did in Yagoona, one suburb next to Bankstown. He was the only son of Vietnamese parents struggling to run a garment-making workshop in Cabramatta and raise Peter and his three sisters. With a deep, stoic sense of determination, he learned to get things done. From the moment we became friends, we both recognised that we shared the same story. Our mothers breathed the same losses and our fathers crafted for us the same quenchable hopes. Peter knew his world was not that of the cocktail parties with the New South Wales Law Society or the cricket club. His world was Cabramatta, hanging out with the boys at the RSL club, hoping to one day pay enough dues to realise for his family their humble dreams. A small home. A new piano for his sister. Nothing grand.

On certain days, whether there was a class or not, Peter would drive into the city in the family's tired red van to deliver finished garments. At times, I would hitch a ride in his van or keep him company on runs to the city. The garments hung off a central rack that ran along the roof, swaying in unison like dancers in a crude group performance, while the coat hangers clinked noisily as he braked for a red light. A few times I went with him to the inner-city studios of well-known Australian fashion designers and waited while Peter picked up a dress sample or negotiated a price for a new load. The studios were often painted all white in a chic minimalist style with clean lines. On one occasion, while waiting for Peter, I sat on a wooden chair by the door watching the designer adjust a new piece on a model, pins in hand. In all the years that my mother had sewn, she never made contact with the designer or label owner. There was a number of layers above us in the production chain, including agents. Peter had decided that since he could speak fluent English and negotiate, his parents could do without agents. My mother refused to allow her children to get involved in her work, for fear it would affect our studies, so I wasn't allowed to take charge like Peter did. The designer/model sighting was a glimpse into another facet of the production chain of which Peter's family, mine and countless others were a part. I thought of my mother, who was probably sewing as I sat there in the inner-city studio. The thoughts of Karl Marx that I had studied in year twelve Economic History formed a glaring frame around the designer/model composition. We were just one of the factors of production.

Often, Peter would pick me up in the red van and drive us around Western Sydney, looking for a place to study. We told each other that it was too noisy and distracting at home because of the sewing machines in our houses, but really we were just procrastinating. We spent nights in empty construction lots in Liverpool inside his van, shifting positions to get sufficient light from the highway. We slept inside the van outside the University of Technology Sydney after the security guards chased us out of the study centres because we weren't students there. Peter tried to coach me in law, in finance, in statistics, but I was constantly distracted by an underlying sense of self-pity. I couldn't fathom how Peter rose above it all and pushed on. Maybe he just had no choice.

•

Away from Sydney University, I spent many happy hours with David and his friends, centred around my giant security blanket of Western Sydney. We would go to Mounties, a community club at Mount Pritchard where, as members, we enjoyed a breakfast buffet for $3.50. The club had more than five hundred poker machines and was rated the highest in the state's poker-machine profit rankings. It was regarded by many as a cultural institution. Every now and then I would cluster around the boys as they played the Cleopatra or Sumo poker machine. The coloured specks of the endless carpet and the electronic tunes of the machines dizzied me.

The boys loved poring over *Hot4s* wheels magazines, ogling the modified sports cars. As I attended car conventions with them, I learned about nitrous oxide, Momo steering wheels, various spoiler dimensions and whether an engine was a rotary. I soon came to love the language of velocity and the freedom in taking a beautiful vehicle to the red line in first gear.

David did Vietnamese martial arts at the Police and Community Youth Club in Cabramatta, as well as tae kwon do in Fairfield. He competed at various venues across the state. I would sit for hours in stadiums, trying to study while waiting for his matches to begin. Sometimes it would be over in the first three minutes. During that brief time while he was on the mat, I held my breath, hands clasped as cheers rose and flared around me. I followed each back kick, front kick, axe kick and punch in a trance-like gaze, brimming with anxiety. As each move sliced the air or thumped the opponent, the ravenous edges of a possible knockout or serious injury clung to my palms. At the end of the rounds, whether he won or lost, relief flooded through me like a cathartic baptism.

Clubs from all over the state competed. Their uniforms were embellished with markings of their clan, their territory whether from Penrith, Kensington or Bankstown. When he wasn't fighting, David would sit with me, identifying key competitors, their fighting styles and weaknesses in a running narrative. There were clubs with predominantly Asian members, others whose members were mainly of Middle Eastern descent and clubs whose membership was a mixed bag. Each competitor had their own preparatory ritual before a fight. Some would find a quiet space to meditate. Others would listen to the *Rocky* theme song.

At the beginning of the competition, the arena was infused with frenzied excitement. Masters and sometimes grandmasters would be present in watchful Mr Miyagi form. There were versions of the Karate Kid pacing about the stadium. People competed for different reasons. Although they came from all over Sydney, when they walked onto the mat wearing their headgear and chest guards, they were simply red or blue. Not Tran, not McGregor, not Habibi, not Kalinowski. Academic, criminal or driving records did not matter. It was in these circles that David discovered a liberating sense of fairness. The arena was a chance to escape the media's scathing representation of Vietnamese men, to block out the death of his uncle and the pain of watching his friends fall. The arena often became his only haven of safety. Of truth.

David's friend Phong had moved out of home to live with his cousin, Bobby, and we would sometimes hang out at their place in Cabramatta. Bobby was a former heroin addict who had been jailed for supply when he was caught dealing drugs to support his habit. As a kid, he, his brother and mother had boarded a small boat with other refugees. Like countless other boats, theirs was attacked by Thai pirates. It is likely that all the women were raped. His mother did not survive. Magically and tragically, the two little boys made it to Australia. For the most part, the two orphans lived on the unforgiving streets, where they found others like themselves. They grouped together. A family by choice. With no one to cradle them, they supported themselves by selling drugs and almost inevitably became addicted to them.

Bobby did his time and got clean in jail. I took to him straight away. His eyes were kind. His crooked teeth and mole on his chin charmed me.

Bobby worked with Phong in a factory in Bonnyrigg, a suburb within the Fairfield local government area. But as things started to disappear from their house, we began to suspect that the white lover had come back to haunt him. Bobby ended up back in jail. His brother, too, spent substantial time in jail, and fell afoul of the stupefyingly inhumane immigration laws. Bobby's brother Matthew was a permanent resident of Australia with a broad ocker accent and only a scant Vietnamese vocabulary. At the time, the government had a policy of deporting permanent residents who were convicted of crimes. This applied no matter how long the resident had been in Australia and no matter how old they were when they arrived. Thus, despite Matthew having spent most of his life in Australia, when the immigration department realised he didn't have Australian citizenship they transferred him from jail into an immigration detention facility to be deported back to Vietnam—a country he had left when he was ten years old. Matthew waited in detention to be sent to a foreign land where he knew no one, where he had no life map and where he had no way back. Ironically, the detention centre was Villawood, the place where my family was clothed and fed and treated with humanity and compassion when we first arrived in this new land. Where we were nourished back to life.

Meanwhile, David's friends were sick of giving second chances to Bobby. He found himself alone and desperate. All of his life, he had held onto one possession that had belonged to his mother: a bracelet. It was his only physical connection to her; a way for him to imagine an embrace from far across the Pacific underneath the stars over the South China Sea. But soon the bracelet found its way to a pawnshop to be placed among other discarded, used jewels. Just for one more hit to seek comfort from this unquestioning mistress, injecting himself somewhere under a cone of light. As the fluid circulated through his body, the wallowing ache of a missing mother and the impending goodbye to his brother would fade.

For a while we didn't know where Bobby was. I knew that he would occasionally drop by an outreach service in Cabramatta, so I went there and gave the street workers a bit of money to buy him some food when he next came by. The last I heard he was doing well. He was clean and had met someone, although his girlfriend's mother disapproved and was doing everything she could to sabotage the relationship.

It's been a long time now. I've lost contact with him and don't know where he is or what he's doing. But I still remember his kind eyes and his crooked, lovely teeth.

Vinh had a friend, Sơn, who lived near us. Sơn and his sister had come to Australia also alone as minors. When I found out about the deportation of permanent residents, I asked Vinh's friend whether he had citizenship. He had no idea. After a few enquiries, we found out that Sơn did not have citizenship. He hadn't known he needed it. He'd been able to get a driver's licence and go to vocational college without it. I urged him to begin the process to get formal citizenship as soon as possible.

On the next Australia Day, Vinh and I accompanied Sơn to the citizenship ceremony at Bankstown Council Chambers. There was no one else to celebrate this day with him. As he stood there, making the Australian Citizenship Pledge among African, Lebanese, Vietnamese and British migrants, I questioned how a nation could sanction the deportation of permanent residents. I looked over at Sơn, a quiet floppy-haired young man with a tender heart who later on would become a bus driver, get married, pay taxes and have a daughter. He would struggle to ensure that his daughter's cleft palate would be repaired. He, like Bobby's brother, had spent his formative years in this country. It seemed to me that as a society we were responsible for him, whether he became a doctor or drug dealer. His failure was our failure. To legislate to deport our disappointments but laud migrant successes as legitimate Australian stories was nothing less than cowardice. The words of Pauline Hanson drifted back to me. *My country. My country.*

•

One evening when David was at my house while I was working on an accounting assignment, he had a call from one of his friends who was in some sort of fight; guys were throwing bricks at him, he said. Immediately, even though he was dressed in his best fake Nautica shirt that I had bought him in Cabramatta, David got into his car to drive the five minutes, past scatterings of fast food joints and petrol stations, down the Hume Highway to Chullora.

I lay on my bed, overcome with helplessness and fear, listening to the hands of the clock ticking and the sound of clinking dishes from the kitchen. My gaze roamed my room restlessly, looking at book titles, at the handles of my drawers, at the red and blue curtains I had sewn myself. I tried to picture the fight scene in my head. Finally David returned. The back of his shirt had been sliced from collar to hem and there was blood on his sleeve from a deep gash on his forearm. He had it stitched up at a clinic that night and the next day we went to university as though nothing unusual had happened.

There were a lot of loose groups around at the time. Some called themselves gangs, some didn't. Some named themselves, some didn't. As far as I knew, only very few were involved in organised crime. Most so-called gangs were just bunches of guys who had something to prove and a confused mix of pride, testosterone and a lack of direction. They would cluster around Bankstown train station with dyed fringes and bad attitudes. Insignificant misunderstandings between the groups where it would be too humiliating to apologise would escalate into feuds. The feuds festered, fed upon themselves and grew into wild centaurs. Sometimes they would be passed onto younger brothers. While in high school, David and his mates used to also sit around at Bankstown train station. They weren't part of a gang, they were just hanging out, sometimes calling out pick-up lines to passing schoolgirls. Some sort of misunderstanding occurred between them and some other guys. Chest-thumping swelled and threats were made. Although time had passed, the tension still simmered and lay like dormant landmines.

I had just got home from class and David and I were about to go out when he got a call. As he held the phone against his ear, I saw his eyes grow wide. The air froze as I recognised the nervous grind of his molars. After he finished the call, he looked at me and said, 'Phong just got shot. I don't have the details. I just have to go.'

I stood in the doorway and watched as David ran to his car. With unflinching precision, he rapidly reversed down the driveway and sped away.

Phong had been shot outside a club in the city. He spent the next three months in hospital. Although he survived, the bullet remained in one of his arteries as the surgeons deemed it too dangerous to operate. The movement of the bullet was unpredictable. Each day that he was alive was a gift. After he got out of hospital, we would sit in his backyard as he told us how he had a tube up his penis most of the time. One of the boys asked whether he got extra sympathy from the nurses and whether they were hot. We laughed and drank VB well into the night. I would witness drunken moments when the boys, almost tearful, would say how thankful they all were to be alive. To be together and to have each other. For all of us, we shared the grit of our working-class Western Sydney lives, the journeys of our parents to this land and the knowledge that more often than not the odds were against us. It forged a solidarity that ran silent and free.

As the media revelled in the drug issues of Vietnamese-dominated Cabramatta, current affairs show *60 Minutes* decided to hold a forum in the heart of darkness. At Cabramatta RSL, lights were set up, boom operators positioned themselves and the host, Ray Martin, checked his hair. People from the local community were invited and strategically placed in certain positions. There were small business owners, and sports and community club representatives. State MP Reba Meagher sat on one side of the room and a representative from the opposition Liberal Party sat on the other. Reba Meagher had been drafted into the seat of Cabramatta by the Labor Party after the shooting of John Newman. She was supposed to represent Cabramatta but she did not live in the area. Instead she lived forty-five kilometres in the expensive beachside suburb of Coogee. The Vietnamese community called her a stepmother.

At the time, I had started to engage in community development with the Vietnamese community, mainly through drug education. Community leaders asked me to attend the televised forum. It would be good to air the perspectives of young people of Vietnamese background. So David and I went along to the event, which was sensationally titled 'Law and Order'. It soon became clear that the forum was carefully scripted, with predetermined questions asked of certain people. The footage was then edited so as to present Cabramatta as a divided community. The theme of law and order—or, it was implied, the lack thereof—meant that the policy response was geared towards a one-dimensional problem, and centred around more police, more cameras and tougher sentencing laws. What a boring, tired and predictable analysis! I was sickened by the transparently political approach. I stood up and volunteered an alternative perspective.

'This is not only a simplified law and order issue. It involves health, education, unemployment, settlement and youth issues. It's more complicated.'

But before I could continue, the host, Ray Martin, interrupted to show the forum video footage of a violent assault captured by closed-circuit television cameras. At the time, nobody realised that the footage had been shot many years earlier. After a small business owner voiced his views about Vietnamese young people, David stood up. His understandable defensiveness hampered his ability to articulate the deeply layered and complex issues facing us. What ensued seemed to be an argument between him and the small business owner. Not surprisingly, this heated confrontation made it into the edited broadcast.

Leaving the forum, David and I felt the same sense of anger and frustration that our voices had been muted. That our community, the Vietnamese community, as well as the Cabramatta community, had become fodder for ratings. We had been manipulated by journalists who wanted to prove themselves brave enough to venture into a politically charged and dangerous part of Sydney. Television producers dramatised community issues and exploited our stories. Our local member of parliament didn't even respect us enough to live in the area she purported to represent. The truth was complex and unsavoury. Nobody wanted to know the truth.

Shortly after the forum, Cabramatta police contacted David and me to see whether we could help them. We met with one of the department heads. She was nice enough and seemed to care about the community and the human face of crime. Maybe they wanted a deeper understanding of some of the issues facing the community. Maybe they wanted intelligence. Either way, I found it hard to overcome my distrust of institutions and authorities governed by the white middle-class majority. Beyond superficial meaningless interactions, I could neither volunteer information nor maintain a relationship with these sweetly sinister organisations. With my artillery of anger, I retreated to my kind and walled myself in.

I'm ashamed to admit that, after the *60 Minutes* broadcast, I was immaturely envious that David got airtime and I didn't. He didn't deserve it. Damn it, I was the one who had always been the social activist. He drank beer on the university lawn while I studied political commentary. With my pride (or ego) wounded, I was unable to see that his voice was as legitimate as mine. It didn't matter that he did not study social science, couldn't quote left-wing theorists or articulate his understanding of rights in a political framework. Leadership required an ability to truly engage, galvanise and involve people like David and his friends. Although I would conduct many workshops with young disillusioned and disadvantaged people in my community development work, in my early twenties I hadn't acquired the heart and humility to truly listen. The irony was that I wanted others to listen to me.

Looking back, I can now understand how I came to connect public achievement and adulation with a sense of self-worth. But at the time, my insatiable hunt for glory was ever present, underlying a genuine commitment to social justice.

As I tried to fight social injustice, meanwhile, I also trudged along painfully at university, a stranger in a strange land. I sat in lecture theatres and tutorials, trying to fade into the walls as my peers asked interesting and thought-provoking questions. On days I had law classes, I felt weighed down by reluctance. I woke up late and ran for the train in the tracksuit pants and oversized T-shirt I'd slept in. Against the backdrop of real-life struggle that I witnessed daily, university seemed like an artificial bubble of fantasy that I couldn't bring myself to care about.

When the results of the first econometrics test were posted, Peter and I joined the crowds around the noticeboards in the Merewether Building to see our scores. Each student scanned the lists for their identification number and accompanying result. Each wore their score on their face as they turned away—some flushed with pleasure, others quietly satisfied, some bewildered. My heart thumped as I looked for my score. Then it was as if my heart stopped. Shock and confusion engulfed me as I turned to look at Peter. I had failed—terribly. I'd been awarded 11 out of 50.

It was clear to me that something was seriously wrong. These results weren't mere ad hoc foibles. As my marks continued to slip I began to question whether I really did have the ability to study at university or for some reason my ability was simply crippled. I began to realise that all my old drive, the focus and determination I had maintained for most of my life, was gone. My former resolve, based on determinable academic objectives, remained in high school while my unworldly self drowned in a massive tertiary world of nameless bodies and unaffordable textbooks. This wasn't an excursion. The mockery of my self-diagnosed sense of displacement in this new world seemed permanent. The trailing adolescent angst had again, finally, caught up with me. Where did I belong? What did I want to do? Where was I going?

My time at Sydney University, especially within the ebb of the conservative law school, had filled me with self-doubt, confirming the existence of a racial and class hierarchy that found me always at the bottom, raising in me questions of place, of identity, of purpose. While others around me had relished their arrival at this bastion of prestige, for me it was an endurance test. I spent each class sitting silently in the last row, shrouded by constant disillusionment. As each lecture, workshop and tutorial passed, I retreated into a shadow that moved unnoticed through the grounds of the university. I pocketed droplets of my peers' conversations, which were peppered with references to their Sydney University lineage. Of grandparents graduating from the same degrees. Of expectations of corporate jobs and yacht club memberships. I didn't matter. I didn't exist. I had never mattered. Not here, not in the media, not on *60 Minutes*, not in the broader political landscape, not in any key locus of decision-making. I never would. Everything was Theirs. The reality cemented itself and burned into me each day like a corrosive acid. In those first few months at university, I waited for permission to exist. But it never came.

CHAPTER 10

A tangible heritage

'I can help you, Cat Thao. We can do this. We can finish this together.' I heard the pleading in his voice but I couldn't bring myself to look at him.

'I can't, Peter. I can't do it anymore.'

'Fuck them, Cat Thao—we can do this.'

After a few months of study, my spirit felt heavy. I was drowning in expectations, in disappointment, in trying to fit in; snapshots from my past and present collided—the parent–teacher meetings, the public-speaking competition, the sewing machines, Vinh's first day at kindergarten, law school tutorials, my father's factory uniform, eating jackfruit in Vietnamese orchards. I made the decision to quit university for that year. I needed space. I needed to recalibrate. I needed to breathe.

I decided to go to Vietnam. This time I would be going alone, as an adult. My family, Peter, and David and his friends came to the airport to say goodbye. David's friends performed a song for me and gave me gifts to remind me to come back. At the time, I didn't know how long I would be away. I cried when David hugged me. Deep down I knew I was afraid—and more so without him. But we both understood that this was something I inexplicably needed to do.

In the end I spent three months in Vietnam, my ascendant curiosity about the country blossoming. The more I discovered, the more I loved it and hungered for more. I spent a lot of time in Gò Dầu with my uncles, aunts and cousins, in the house where my mother had spent her childhood. I played soccer with kids in a dusty ground fenced off by a crumbling wall. I went to the market with my aunt to buy live chickens and freshly skinned jumping frogs. I rode a motorbike at dusk past acres of rubber-tree forests, until darkness descended along with a mammoth swarm of moths that smacked into my face. The air was scented with simplicity and carried aromas of star anise, garlic and fried fish. People sold petrol on the side of the street in old two-litre Coke bottles. Buffaloes and cows trundled along worn paths, pulling carts of freshly harvested rice. In the evenings, villagers ate on the floor in mud huts, drinking homemade rice wine.

One night we celebrated my birthday. My cousins and kids from the village gathered in my grandfather's house, in front of the ancestral altar. Techno music pumped and I taught the kids how to dance while the smaller ones ate cake. My grandfather, who was gradually becoming deaf, observed us with an indulgent smile.

My cousins and I went to orchards and sat on woven grass mats surrounded by fruit trees, eating lychees and longans until our bellies ached.

I rode on the back of my cousin's motorbike, moving along the narrow path separating my grandfather's rice fields until my cousin, bike and I slipped into the field, emerging wet and muddy. The farmers laughed heartily at our silliness while the ducks looked on.

One evening my aunt took me on her motorbike and we trundled along unsealed roads, swerving around pot holes and overgrown grass. The sun was hanging low in the sky and the fresh smell of earth and farm surrounded us. Finally we arrived at an old house that was surrounded by wild foliage and tall coconut trees that were bent and swaying slightly. It was clear that no one lived there.

'Your dad was born here,' she told me. 'He lived in this house. Your grandfather planted those coconut trees.'

I stared at the old house. Its wood panelling was dark and patchy with moisture. I walked over to the coconut trees and ran my fingers over the shrapnel wounds it had sustained. Here I was on the land of my father's father, the land that had nurtured my father as a child like an external womb. I breathed in the air. I pulled at the grass. I basked in the red sun. I clung to the tree, hoping my heritage would stream into me—this physical connection to something real. A connection to this majestic and tangible heritage. I kept my hand on one of the coconut trees for a while. I felt its roughness and imagined my father as a young boy and his father watching him many years ago—before war, before separation.

In Vietnam, I was far from Redfern station, from essays on crime and punishment, far from classes punctuated with conversations of boat clubs I would never go to. And far from a country where I had no continuity of place. And I didn't want to let go.

•

Towards the middle of my trip, I went with a group of college students on a four-day bus journey to central Vietnam. I stayed at a beautiful, serene pebble beach. The locals told me stories of how, in the late 1970s, people would come to the beach each day to remove refugees' bodies that had washed ashore and give them proper ceremonial death rites. They told me of people who scanned the beach every day for belongings of loved ones who had departed without a trace, searching for answers, for finality among the same pebbles that I was walking upon. A shirt, a watch, a button.

At night, the college students built a camp fire and sang. I didn't know any Vietnamese songs so I sang the first part of 'Stand By Me'. They clapped along joyfully. The jubilant flames cast flickering shadows on our faces, moving and jumping like a mad puppet show. These were the types of memories I had hoped I would create during my university years back in Sydney.

We all slept on hammocks on the beach. I listened to the waves and felt the ocean breeze as I fell asleep under a sky dense with stars, dreaming of lost things.

I also visited the romantic mountain city of Dalat in the Central Highlands. With its cool European climate, it was a favoured holiday destination of the French during their colonial occupation of Vietnam. Dotted around this beautiful city were old French villas nestled in pine trees, waterfalls and cobblestone laneways. Giant lakes and silhouettes of mountain ranges were the backdrop for little mobile cafés with low plastic chairs.

I was told by a bus driver that there was a table near a Chinese temple in Dalat that could spin upon command. Apparently it was made of an ancient wood that was now extinct. There were three tables in the world made from these trees that now only existed on the tongues and in the minds of bus drivers and villagers. As I walked uphill towards the Chinese temple, there was a humble house on the right. I took off my shoes and went inside. The living room was small and there was a guest book on the table. Not much was exchanged between myself and the woman who served me tea, except warm smiles. She then led me to the round table. It was not grand by any means, being only seventy centimetres or so in diameter and standing only a metre high. There was no gloss or decorative elements of any kind. The woman told me to place both hands on the table and then either say aloud or think to myself the word 'spin'. I put my hands on the table and thought, *Spin right, spin right.* Then, ever so gently, the table began to move anticlockwise. I then thought, *Stop*. The table complied. *Spin to the left, faster, faster*, I commanded silently. Again, the table did as I'd instructed. The woman then removed the table-top from its base and placed it on the ground to demonstrate that there was no trick, no hidden wires. It was utterly and unassumingly spectacular. My father had always told me that our ancestors reside in the trees, in the rivers and the mountains. Here, in this simple house, a demonstration of Vietnamese mysticism revealed itself to me. Ancient. Inexplicable. Present.

•

A few of my cousins were living in Ho Chi Minh City, studying and working. One evening, when Vietnam won a soccer match in a notable Asian competition, my cousin asked whether I wanted to ride around the city with her. I had no idea of the scene I was about to witness. The streets of the city exploded with euphoric energy, its veins rupturing into a sea of red flags. The mayhem of thousands of roaring motorbikes, each with young teenagers, grandparents and couples with babies banging together saucepan lids and plastic bottles, transformed the city into a throbbing chamber of mass patriotism. Those who weren't riding motorbikes stood on balconies above the streets waving flags, bashing wooden chopsticks against pots, chanting, 'Vietnam undefeated! Vietnam undefeated!' On the back of my cousin's Honda Dream motorbike, stuck in traffic, gridlocked on Le Loi Boulevard, both my knees almost touching the knees of other Vietnamese people on either side of me sitting on the backs of motorbikes. Smiles beamed from every face, wrinkled and new. As the crescendos of chants swept through the crowds like a swift monsoon rain, I saw the people's aspirations buoy them. Awaken them. Nourish them. I felt a sense of shared identity. At last I was one of Us. I looked at the people beside me and in front of me, at all the people on a tide of motorbikes that never ended. Everyone looked like me. I felt liberated by my insignificance. And I felt membership. A membership that would never be questioned. I promised myself that one day I would come back here to live, to belong and to be free.

At the end of the trip, I went back to my aunt's house, where my father's mother lived. My aunt asked me to go with her into one of the bedrooms. As I sat on the bed, she took out a few bits of paper from a drawer inside the wardrobe. She began to tell me about the time when my father decided to leave Vietnam. My uncle, his younger brother, had gone first, by boat. After some time, they had arrived in Australia.

'When your father left, I asked him to take my son, your cousin. If he had stayed, he could have been forced to join the military or he would be sent far away. No one had any idea about the fate of young able men after the war ended. Your father definitely would have been punished further, if not killed. When he left, we heard nothing for a long time. If it was safe, we were all going to go. We had no idea whether they were dead or alive. We waited and waited, trying to soothe our anxieties with daily empty rituals. Then we received a letter, smuggled to us.'

My aunt showed me the note, now over twenty years old. Only a few lines were written on it. It was my father's unmistakable handwriting, elegant and bold.

We are safe now. Extremely perilous. Do not leave.

I sank to the cold tiled floor, leaning against the wooden bed.

The urgency and fear in those words brought to me the image of a man who had barely survived. A man who had no idea about his own future and that of his nephew, wife and baby, one of their kin already lost deep in the jungles of Cambodia. I felt a sharp ache in my chest as I contemplated the fear my parents had faced, the brutality and muzzled pain they had endured. As I cried softly I thought, *I am a witness.*

The noise from my aunt's rice mill churned incessantly like swirls of ocean foam. My aunt left to attend to some rice buyers. Alone in that room, with the old pre-war ceiling fan spinning, I stroked the paper. I was holding a physical connection to a young man who had bravely set off into an unimaginable future. A young man I longed to know. *We are safe now.*

•

After I arrived back in Australia, I found myself driving through Chester Hill past a large empty park. After the noise and colour of Vietnam, the silence of the wide streets and blankness of the sparse parks made me melancholy. I longed for the earthy gestures of farmers and the frenzied mania of a bustling nation. I missed my aunts' excessive fretting and the daily intrusion into everyone else's business like it was their right. Compared to the dense stew of Vietnam, the suburban and urban landscapes of Sydney seemed like a desolate graveyard.

With a few more months before the university year started again, I applied for some jobs. I eventually landed an entry-level claims-processing job at a large superannuation fund administrator. Excited to work in my first white-collar job in a tall city building, I purchased a cheap pale grey suit and cream shoes from Bankstown shopping centre. Although I didn't know it at the time, it was very much a New Girl Look. But soon after I started I grew insanely bored of entering data and reading through endless claim sheets. I gravitated towards the IT helpdesk guys and found myself thinking of ways to pass time. Once, I forgot to switch my mobile phone to silent and it rang loudly. The manager spoke to my supervisor, who in turn was asked to advise me on appropriate office etiquette. Such was the world of polite water-cooler conversation and stifled whispers between workstations.

When I received my first pay cheque, I decided to treat myself and David to a buffet lunch at the Sheraton on the Park, where I'd had my year twelve school formal. It was the only five-star hotel I had ever set foot in. As I moved cautiously around the food stations, a bowl with a ladle caught my eye. As I spooned the clear broth into a bowl, David came up and looked at it suspiciously. 'I don't know if that's soup.' I blushed, embarrassed, when we realised it was the container for the dirty ladle. In Vietnamese cuisine soup was normally a clear broth and so I thought the slightly murky water that the ladle was resting in was the soup.

The actual soup was in a tureen next to it. We suppressed our laughter as we shuffled back to our table, surrounded by a battalion of unfamiliar cutlery.

By the time the new university year started, I had had enough of being a cog in a giant mundane wheel of corporate routine. At orientation week, I weaved through the university club stands while the music from the band on the stage blared. Beer was drunk in great quantities from plastic cups while boys kicked footballs around on the lawn. I passed the Anime Club, Drinking Society and Evangelical Union among many others. When I found the Vietnamese Students Association I immediately became a member.

I enrolled in the same compulsory subjects. Accounting, economics, econometrics, Legal Institutions and Law, Lawyers and Justice. Somehow after returning from Vietnam, I possessed greater resolve. The paper that I turned in for Legal Institutions received the top mark and was copied and distributed as a model for all the other law students. All without going to the Intensive English Language Centre. I proffered comments in class on the moral philosophy implications of Jeremy Bentham's panopticon. I debated the administration of justice. I wrote great essays in macroeconomics. However, it wasn't long before the old feelings of isolation returned. I decided once again on a policy of disengagement with the law faculty and the student body. I attended only the minimum requirement of classes. In all my years at law school, I never once attended the weekly level five cocktail gatherings at the St James Campus in the city.

I had a friend of Iranian background who was studying for the same double degree. He was funny, politically astute and had a sharp sense of self. I met a few others who were nice enough, but none who would become good friends.

I started to become heavily involved in the Vietnamese Students Association. There were barbecues and fundraisers out in Bankstown or Cabramatta. I was one of the masters of ceremonies for a large Christmas ball that raised funds for Vietnamese refugees in a camp in the Philippines. Very quickly, I was recruited by the executive board of the official Vietnamese Community Organisation. The main office in John Street, Cabramatta, administered a range of programs funded by various state government departments, including arts and health. Under the guidance of the elected executive, the office employees coordinated community activities such as the annual Tết Festival as well as the occasional protest against political delegations from Communist Vietnam. There was a variety of Vietnamese community organisations, such as the senior citizens group, the Vietnamese Buddhist Society, the Vietnamese Catholic Society, the Vietnamese Women's Association, the Vietnamese Scouts Group and the Vietnamese Students Association.

All these groups were eligible to vote for the executive of the official umbrella Vietnamese Community Organisation in Australia, New South Wales chapter. Anyone in the community could also register to vote. There were election ads run on Vietnamese radio and in print during the election campaigns. Each chapter executive nominates representatives to form the federal executive. Whichever group won the chapter elections, there was always a guarantee that all the core activities of the organisations revolved around pro-democracy campaigns for Vietnam.

•

The anniversary of the fall of Saigon had arrived. Every 30 April, each chapter of the Vietnamese Community Organisation in Australia sent members on a pilgrimage to Canberra to commemorate the day. Countless free buses from Victoria, New South Wales and other states made their way to the front of the Vietnamese embassy in Canberra to mourn the loss of the war and protest against the current regime's atrocities. People made protest signs and waved them along with the old South Vietnamese flag. A flag which within Vietnam is not only offensive but is buried along with the official version of history. Men who still had their medals and insignia would wear them with pride. The old fed the young with stories of horror and injustice. Musicians sang old pro-Saigon war songs while fists pumped in the air after the leaders yelled, 'Down with Communism!'

In the first year that I participated in the fall of Saigon pilgrimage, I roamed the crowd taking photos. The image of one particular man struck me. He was small with a long thin face, high cheekbones and round eyes sunk into two oversized sockets. He looked like a man-mouse. But his face wasn't what drew my attention. It was the way he stood. He was resolute and proud, unflinching in the audience as speeches and songs continued throughout the afternoon. He clasped the pole of a flag with his right hand, resting it almost vertically against him. His stance remained unchanged for a long time. Nobody came to talk to him or stand with him. His reverent silence exuded a noble sadness that moved me deeply. As I looked through the lens of my camera at him, I tried to imagine his story and the thoughts that were mulling inside him. Where had he come from in Vietnam? Did he have any family? How did he get to Australia? How many others like him were there?

This man stood quietly among other old soldiers, now with greying beards and calluses on their palms from driving forklifts, containing the memories and conviction reserved for this annual release. It was an emotional display of a community's grief that was far from subsiding. Just like revolutionary causes all around the world throughout the ages, indifferent to the currency of the political ideology, the young were central to the potency and continuity of the cause. We were needed to ensure that even as time passed, the cause remained. The war was not over until it was won, however long it took. It was our duty not to forget, to honour our parents and those who had not survived. The Communist Party of Vietnam was composed of a bunch of corrupt selfish officials who exploited their own people. It was a despotic regime. The sea of yellow flags raised sombrely before me now was a direct antithesis to the celebratory exuberant streams of red-starred flags I had ridden among only a year earlier. I didn't know how to reconcile my feelings of membership with knowing that the Vietnam I had visited and loved, where I had felt a powerful sense of belonging, was a country my family had fled. But that year I learned the power and meaning of a flag. That it can transform into a weapon, become a robe of glory, an epitaph or a constant reminder of defeat.

When Sydney hosted the Olympics, David and I watched Vietnam win its first-ever Olympic medal. A woman from Nha Trang, on the South Central Coast of Vietnam, won silver in tae kwon do. There was no one from the Vietnamese Australian community visible in the audience. International students from Vietnam had come to support the fighter, bringing with them the national flag. Their faces were painted red with a yellow star. They cheered loudly from the stands as they witnessed a unique moment in Vietnamese history. The international students erupted into proud but disbelieving screams, even though the fighter missed out on the gold medal. At the end we had our photos taken with the silver medallist.

A couple of weeks later, when my uncle was at our house, I described the wonderful event. My uncle had been a naval officer of the South Vietnamese government. Usually jovial, his manner was curt as he said, 'It's been reported in our community newspapers that the girl was bought off and deliberately lost the match.'

'How can you trust the intelligence behind this news?' I retorted. 'Propaganda can be propagated by both sides.'

I took out the photos to show him, hoping that he would be proud of Vietnam's achievement. The pictures showed

David and I posing with the medallist, who was holding up the Communist flag.

'You should be ashamed!' my uncle thundered. 'How could you have stood there with her? It isn't just a flag. Flags are not just symbols. We bled for our flag! We died for our flag! That red flag represents a victory stolen from us, mocking our humiliation, spitting on our fallen brothers in unmarked graves. Shame! Shame! What would the leaders of the community say if they saw these photos! You will destroy us!'

My face burned with confusion and naivety. I buried the photos at the bottom of my desk drawer and never looked at them again.

Throughout the years I was involved with the Vietnamese community, I learned freedom songs and the old South Vietnam Republican anthem—all banned in Vietnam now. I learned the supposed duty of young Vietnamese in our diaspora communities to rescue our brethren back in Vietnam from human rights abuses and Communism. I went to camps and surrounded myself with people who looked like me, spoke like me and told me of a greater purpose. They told me of honour, of cultural pride, of legacy, of reason. I drank in this newfound sense of belonging like a thirsty traveller in the desert. I went with the chapter president to political party dinners and press conferences and to meetings with all those who needed to woo the Vietnamese community, whether they were chasing votes or a tabloid story. I chatted with Gough Whitlam, former Australian prime minister, spoke at Parliament House on the thirty-fifth anniversary of the fall of Saigon, shook hands with future Australian prime minister Kevin Rudd, and went to Canberra with a delegation to present to the bipartisan Amnesty International Parliamentary Committee. I facilitated community workshops on the challenges facing Vietnamese children and parents, from drugs and the language barrier to generational and cultural conflict. I sat on the National Community Advisory Committee to the SBS. I was on the management board of the New South Wales Ethnic Communities' Council—the peak non-government organisation for ethnic communities in the state. I attended countless consultations, listened to the woes of detainees in immigration detention and presented proposals for drug education reform in Canberra.

I kept overly busy with community development work, distracting myself from the loneliness I felt at university. But no matter what, at least I had David. We were still dating. While I was immersed in my community development work, David and his buddies had all bought motorbikes. The crew adored their bikes. They rode up and down the coast, and spent hours cleaning them and posing with them for photos. David would pick me up on his bike and take me to university.

We were in love. It wasn't the expressive type of love I saw in the movies, with excessive handholding and physical affection—we were Asian, after all—but we had a deep sense of shared history and silent understanding. It was love first-generation-migrant style.

As I progressed into second year at university, I became president of the Sydney University Vietnamese Students Association. It was the year of the biannual international Vietnamese youth conference, and it was being held in Paris. All the other university Vietnamese student associations in Australia raised funds to subsidise the trip. There were concerts at Bankstown Town Hall, fashion parades in Cabramatta and raffle tickets sold to almost every Vietnamese parent and relative in Australia. Despite the fundraising efforts, I knew it was impossible for me to go. My Centrelink allowance was just enough to cover my books, train tickets and food; I had nothing to spare.

One afternoon, as David and I sat on the steps in my backyard watching the landlords' kid play, he asked, 'Do you really want to go?'

'I feel like I should because I'm the president. I really want to go.'

'Okay.'

The next day David put an ad in the paper to sell his beloved Honda Fireblade. Then he gave me the money to go to Paris.

The cheapest ticket involved flying from Sydney to Melbourne to Hong Kong to Japan to Russia to Paris. I travelled as part of a group of about thirty people who constituted the Australian Vietnamese delegation. The leg to Russia was on an Aeroflot flight. An Aeroflot plane had crashed only a week earlier. I didn't need to know this but one of the other students kept mentioning it. The tray table was broken and kept smacking my knees throughout the flight. None of the flight attendants smiled. To help with my anxiety, another delegate in the group gave me a sleeping pill. It completely knocked me out. When I awoke, I had a thick pool of drool on my shirt and the plane had landed. The Russian passengers clapped and cheered loudly as we shuffled off the plane—to discover that our connecting flight had been cancelled. So the Australian delegation sprawled across the floor of the Moscow airport for a few hours while we waited for someone to give us directions. We avoided eye contact with the rather gruff airport staff who strode briskly around the airport. Eventually they put us up in a nearby hotel to wait for a flight the next day. It was summer in Russia, and I was enthralled by the idea that the sun never went completely down. I stood at the window for hours, marvelling at the white and still night.

Hundreds of young people of Vietnamese descent from sixteen countries congregated in Paris. Each delegation contributed a piece to the opening ceremony of the conference, whether it was a comedic parody of a famed Vietnamese variety show or a moving protest song. For the week of the conference, we met with people who spoke Vietnamese with Norwegian, French and British accents. We exchanged stories of growing up as refugees in our host countries. We laughed, we sang, we understood. There were lectures and presentations on ways to bring democracy to Vietnam, on the role of art in the movement. A Vietnamese international student with inside information on how the Communist Party monitored its people apparently risked much to talk to us. I don't remember what he said but I remember the security controls: once we were all seated in the theatre, the screens on the windows were electronically rolled down until there was no more natural light and no one from outside could see in.

In a plenary workshop, a question was asked of us: what did it mean to be Vietnamese? Resilience. Excellence. Achievement. I raised my hand but posed questions instead of giving a response. I said that it was easy to think of the apparent successes of our community as a manifestation of what it means to be Vietnamese. But what of our brothers and sisters who suffered from drug addiction, or were involved in crime? Did we still think of them as Vietnamese? Did they possess the core of Vietnamese identity? I was aware of how privileged we were to be there, that we were mostly university students with the means to travel to Europe. But we shouldn't forget the nameless others back home who were not so lucky. I thought our community development initiatives needed to look beyond the present pro-democracy speak.

The room next to the plenary theatre had been transformed into an exhibition space. During the lunch break I went inside to view the works. I was transported back home to a worn mother and long nights. On display was the work of a Vietnamese Australian photographer from Melbourne who'd photographed the sewing rooms in a number of Vietnamese homes. There were no people in the photos; instead of the usual sense of urgent activity, the rooms were eerily still as though they had violently sucked out leaving a vacuum. They were solemn chambers emanating a grave life of their own. The piles of garments frozen under a stark halogen light were too familiar. The image of Jesus Christ with His illuminating sacred heart and compassionate eyes on the wall could have been ours. So could the chopsticks that rested on a bowl of instant noodles, beckoning an increasing call to work. Thousands of miles away, on a different continent, these photographs both comforted and confronted me. This was my story on the walls and the photographer challenged me to embrace it. He delivered to me the type of validation that comes with a published artwork carrying the core themes of one's life. He saw me. It was an acknowledgement I had long needed. As I fell into these pictures, I wept grateful tears of recollection and relief. In that little room in Paris, it was the beginning of my understanding of the transformative and healing powers of creative art. It was a lesson I would never forget.

At the closing ceremony of the conference, a symbolic flag was handed over to the Canadian delegation, who would host the conference in two years' time. As the music played and the delegates clapped, our spirits soared. It was summer in Paris and we were an international body of bright young students bound by a common heritage, by one race.

On Bastille Day, we roamed the streets of the city and took a boat ride on the Seine, waving huge yellow and red-striped flags. In hindsight, it was bizarre that we chose another nation's day of pride to display ours. Nevertheless, riding on a high of unity and belonging, we celebrated.

•

My time in Paris solidified in me a forceful commitment to Vietnamese people—a commitment which, at the time, felt like a natural responsibility. Beyond the uplifting celestial songs, the rhetoric and flag-waving, I wanted to examine political structures within the framework of development economics and capitalism. I wanted to explore the holistic merits of democracy for nations like Vietnam. I wanted to understand human rights in the context of globalisation. So upon my return to Sydney, I decided to discard my finance major in my Bachelor of Commerce and switch to government and international relations.

It was an intellectually rewarding choice. Finance's random walk theory mattered much less to me than duty. But as I sat in lectures and researched for assignments, I began to see that the sentiments of the Vietnamese community were based more on hurt than rational or considered argument; that the political agenda to restore Vietnam had a lot to do with communal and individual journeys for redemption and healing as well as corrosive bitterness, robed in noble and righteous aspiration. How does one erase the memory of burying a fellow soldier alive at the order of a North Communist cadre? How does someone who is forced to flee his homeland after spending years in a re-education camp overcome the sight of his wife being raped by pirates? I would never have the answers for these men and women. I would never be able to heal all my father's wounds. But maybe I could learn to see through the present to the forgotten pre-war days, to look past the unfathomable journeys of hurt to the man he once had been. Maybe, ever so slightly, like a feather scraping the air, I could help to heal these deep, deep wounds.

CHAPTER 11

So much world

In my third year of university, when a new president was elected to the Vietnamese Students Association my participation in Vietnamese community activities waned in favour of broader community development and arts projects. As I initiated and managed statewide projects, I began to see how similar minority groups are to each other. The stories had the same themes of dispossession, of trauma, of persecution, of survival. I witnessed the magical ability of the arts to empower and to change nightmares into dreams. With the notions of advocacy and storytelling, I busied myself. I exhibited as a multimedia artist in various exhibitions, won a film scholarship and performed as a spoken-word artist at the Museum of Sydney. I initiated a multicultural short film festival and worked with the Ethnic Communities' Council to establish its first youth awards. Study for my double degree continued but not without difficulty as my attentions were diverted. Law interested me less than reading Plato's *Republic* and the real changes that I saw effected in my extracurricular work. Peter continued to feed me notes and pass me down tutorial guides. The busier I grew, the more I was distracted from underlying feelings of shame and disassociation.

During this time, our family moved from Chester Hill to a cheap and decaying house in Bankstown. The lawn at the front was unkempt and there was an old tyre and other bits of junk underneath a frangipani tree that grew carelessly against the fence. The dated white fibro house boasted a threatening BEWARE OF DOG sign on the side gate, but there was no dog. Underneath my bedroom window a couple of forgotten rose bushes grew. As I lay on my bed on windy nights they would scratch at the window like a forgotten puppy. On the day we moved in, we found a couple of discarded syringes at the foot of the rose bushes. Inside, the green paisley carpet was dotted with cigarette burns. The kitchen was painted a crude, dated blue. The bathroom walls featured a couple of sad raised goldfish and shells. We froze in the winter and sweltered in the summer.

The Vietnamese landlord lived at the back with his young family in a tiny burrow covered by corrugated iron. We weren't far from the stretch of Canterbury Road where the prostitutes would position themselves in the evenings. The side streets were known for drop-offs and exchanges of drugs. It wasn't uncommon to see police cars meandering through these streets at night. Before we bought a shed to store the meagre hoard of belongings we had accumulated over two decades, Vinh slept in the living room on the couch. But despite all its shortcomings, with rents on the rise we were just happy to have found a place near public transport and a church.

Before we moved to Bankstown, my parents had decided to sell our sewing machines. Business was drying up as the low-end work was being shifted to countries with cheap labour—such as Vietnam, ironically. My mother no longer had the visual precision to work on the higher end, more meticulously designed smaller loads. In any case, there wasn't going to be enough room for the machines in the new place. Their departure marked the end of a chapter in our settlement journey. From the time I began preschool to when I entered university, the two machines were reliable friends to us: the training wheels of a young refugee family. The pair should have been used by both my mother and Hồng Khanh, her youngest brother who was lost in Cambodia. I was sure her heartache gnawed her softly as she sewed and thought of her lost baby brother.

On the day the machines left us, I looked at them for a long time before they were moved into the truck. The yellow measuring tape stuck along the edge of the Singer machine was peeling. Its numbers had partially faded. The pedal of the overlocker had worn away, exposing a patch of raw shiny metal where, for two decades, my mother's foot moved in sure pulses. The sound of the machines that welcomed me each time I opened the front door was the sound of rent money, school fees and grocery shopping. They had sustained us.

As I traced the lines of the machines that day, I remembered a time in class at law school. The girl I sat next to had thin lips, long hair and wore expensive black-framed glasses. She had perfect teeth and skin. No visible pores. After several classes and a few polite conversations during break times, I asked her what she wanted to do after university. At the time, my mother had been sewing regularly for an urban fashion label that had stores in almost every large shopping centre in Sydney. We had been going through a steady head contractor based out of Chester Hill, whose kids I tutored in English and economics. My fellow student told me that she was going to work for her family's business after she graduated.

'What sort of business is it?' I asked.

'We have a fashion label.' She told me the name. It was the same label my mother was sewing for. The two words by themselves were just harmless nouns. But as they left her mouth, I felt a wrenching stab. It was a bitter reinforcement of my rank in the world order.

Not long after this conversation, I received a grant to write a play. *Living Room* was based on my mother's experience inside our various sewing rooms and how, from a seat at the sewing machine, she watched her daughter grow. Maybe it was an attempt to validate her experiences and my own. But at the time, I had no such lucid intentions. On opening night at Parramatta Riverside Theatre, there was a light buzz. The audience was a mixture of friends, family, artists, producers and media. This time, I didn't need to translate for her. Quiet tears gently flowed down her cheeks as she saw her life played out on stage by a Filipino actress. The play ran for all of ten minutes, which I would later feel was an insult. I sat beside her in the audience, squeezing her hand. 'Understand?' 'Understand.' She smiled graciously. Forgiving me.

Later that week, I sat in class with the fashion-label pore-less-skin student. As the lecturer droned on, again I found my mind sauntering in and out of the classroom. Were our destinies already forged? I wondered. Did any of this matter? With increased vigour, I began pursuing grant applications and scholarships to produce artworks. This was the arena where I found clear meaning and salvation. A world where I could control storylines and outcomes.

I received a grant from the Literature Board of the Australia Council for the Arts to produce a writing and photography anthology, *Memory Frame*. A friend and I gathered together a small group of young Vietnamese Australians to reflect on their families' journeys to Australia and their ultimate conception of place and identity. For my contribution, I sifted through the scant collection of photos from the refugee camp and interviewed my father. Holding my list of prepared questions, I sat with him at the dining table donated to us by our former landlord. The yellow plastic tablecloth with blue tulips reflected the sun shining through the kitchen window, draped in a jungle themed curtain. I asked my father about the decision to leave Vietnam, about what he remembered of the journey through Cambodia, about the disappearance of my uncle. A few minutes after we'd begun, he asked me to stop and then he left the room. 'Later.' But later did not come.

The next morning my father said he'd found it hard to sleep, and when he did the nightmares came. The steam from the instant coffee rose from the Bankstown City Council mug as he spoke. Underneath the Vietnamese Students Association cap I had given him, my father looked old. I had no words of comfort to offer him. But I felt a sordid shame and remorse at the realisation that I had been so insensitive in pursuit of my 'project'. His memories were vivid. I recalled one year we had attended an Australia Day event organised by the local council at a park. There was a Blackstone engine. It took my father back to the very night he, his wife and young baby had spent on a roadside underneath the black Cambodian sky across from an abandoned Blackstone factory. Without considerion, I had turned the interview into an intellectual fact-finding exercise that assaulted him like an icy ten-page hospital questionnaire in English. I marvelled at my own immaturity.

My mother told me that she would answer any questions I had. 'Dad is fragile. He is a lot weaker than you think.'

But even as I asked my mother a watered-down version of my original set of questions, I could not shake my disgust at myself for causing my beloved father so much pain. I pictured tormenting images of jungles, guns, uniforms and savage eyes hovering above my parents' bed like a torrent of ghouls. I wanted to know where these images had come from. What scenes of horror had he witnessed? What patches of happiness had been robbed from him? What decay had he seen? No matter how many questions I had, I knew now that the answers I sought could not come from my father himself. It was only through fragments of stories that my mother and relatives told over time that I was able to piece together a jigsaw collection of my family history. Incomplete, but just enough.

From the time we moved to Bankstown, I developed a passionate attachment to the community. It is one of the most culturally diverse areas in Australia, home to a sizeable community of Vietnamese and Lebanese migrants. Bankstown was the subject of a series of damaging media reports focusing on gang violence, attempts to shoot police and race-related gang rape. I sat on the inaugural youth advisory committee of the city council. In our meetings at the council chambers beside Paul Keating Park, the committee members would often share stories that had outraged each of us. There were instances where reporters handed out baseball caps to willing youths at the station in order to photograph them, instructing them to pose with infamous American manufactured gang gestures in exchange for a small amount of money. When the story ran with the image, the headline featured the fear-inducing word 'gang'.

As young people of a misunderstood community, we tried hard to advocate for truth, for social justice. But as reports were churned out by journalists sentenced to community news-paperdom before moving up the Fairfax/News Corp ladder, many of us became more watchful and more distrustful of outsiders as well as a mainstream Australia that saw our diversity as a threat to their 'way of life'. Within the streets of Bankstown, I learned to feel comfortable and proud in a place where in the main shopping centre women in hijab walked among Asian families and African youths without people turning their heads or clutching their purses.

As I commuted from our fibro house in Bankstown to the glossy central business district of Sydney, I felt I was crossing a border between two different countries. A pensive frustration continued to mushroom inside me. Postcodes still mattered.

Some of the law subjects I was taking required me to attend the St James campus in the city. It was a tall, narrow, claustrophobic building in the heart of the Sydney law precinct, opposite the Supreme Court of New South Wales. Like the other law offices and courts built in the late 1960s, the law school's grey concrete walls were cold and forbidding. In the small brown-tiled foyer, a long noticeboard sat inside a glass case mounted on the wall facing the lifts. This was where faculty news, paralegal jobs and information on research grants and scholarships were displayed. On level five of the building a small shop sold pies, sandwiches and drinks in a communal area with a few couches, tables and a pool table. I hardly ever went up there. If I did, it was to buy a cup of barely tolerable coffee or use the bathroom. While I would wait for the lady to make the coffee, I watched the other students assemble in cosy clusters on the couches, sharing notes and chatting. I knew I would never be one of them.

I spent as little time as I could in the suffocating building of law school. The long neon lights were invasive and the gargoyles that towered above the city on the building's corners grimaced at me with sadistic pity. I floated in and out of the shadows of the back rows in class. But a few redeeming moments occurred each time I alighted the train at St James station. I would walk through a tunnel and emerge into the beautiful expanse of Hyde Park. Often the buskers and homeless would be stationed just before the stairs ascended onto the street level. One busker, who I befriended, played the clarinet and as I walked into the tunnel each time, the gradual pitch of his tunes would fill and soothe me like a cup of peppermint and honey tea. At lunchtimes, I would escape the drab spell of law school and lie sprawled across the grass of Hyde Park, watching a game of giant chess or children feeding pigeons near the naked statues at the central fountain. When I had a late class, I loved walking through the archway of giant towering trees that latticed its branches together at the top in a mystical apex of enchanted green.

One evening, as I walked through Hyde Park, the fairy lights flickered and blinked among the trees as the sun swiftly descended. I dumped my bag at the foot of a tree and climbed up. I sat like a hidden insect, recording the suits going home and parents with strollers against shimmering wishing pools of water. It was the cusp of spring and Louis Armstrong streamed through my iPod against the five o'clock Elizabeth Street traffic. I wanted to dissolve right there. After a year of classes at the St James campus, I was miserable and found the prospect of a further two years full-time there unbearable. (My self-imposed isolation probably didn't help.) I couldn't bear the ritualistic, tortuous attendance at the St James campus. I saw drones without imagination posing as students. I toyed with the idea of taking another deferment.

One evening, I kneeled in front of the altar in our living room. I had in my hand two twenty-cent coins and a plate; I needed to pray and ask a question. One head and one tails meant yes. The Venetian blinds trembled as the house reverberated to the rumble of the semitrailers that roared along the main road outside. I lit an incense stick and asked my grandmother whether I should defer university or not. I climbed onto a chair and planted the incense stick in the cup of uncooked rice at the Virgin Mary's feet. I tossed the coins onto the plate. One head and one tails. My grandmother had spoken. The next day I unenrolled from university.

Soon after, I got a job with a Western Sydney local government as a project consultant. Over the next few years I would work as a project manager and consultant to various public and private sector organisations. I also continued my community work in youth development. That year, I saw an ad on a youth website for the position of National Youth Representative to the United Nations General Assembly in New York City. I decided to apply, unaware of what it really entailed. There were applications from across Australia and several rounds of interviews. The United Nations Youth Association, in conjunction with the Department of Foreign Affairs, would select one person to represent Australia over several months at the United Nations General Assembly in New York City. The mandate was to work with the United

Nations Secretariat, other country missions and delegates to advocate for the issues of young people in Australia and beyond.

While I worked at my job as a project consultant, I continued to tutor in the evenings and work as a freelance artist. When I had saved enough money, I told my parents that I thought it was time for them and Vinh to go to Vietnam. Văn and I would cover all the costs, including the cartons of Eagle Brand medicated oil for all the relatives and neighbours. The last time Vinh had been to Vietnam he was two years old. Now he was fifteen. He felt no emotional connection to our extended family and the country of his parents' birth. He only knew them through a skimpy collection of photos and memories from that maiden trip in 1991. He only remembered Vietnam as being dirty. It was thirteen years since my mother's last visit and eleven years for my father. The trip was long overdue. Such time and distance was thinning their native fires and wilting their spirits. And so my parents and Vinh went to Vietnam while I stayed in Sydney.

The night before they left, my mother was fretting over the luggage, packing and unpacking again. I felt her nervous anticipation. I knew they were grateful to go back, but I knew my father's sense of shame. It was close to twenty-five years since they left Vietnam and their pockets weren't deep. They had no wealth to speak of. The gifts for ageing relatives and old friends would be limited. The visit would be bittersweet. My mother weighed the last of the bags.

'Are you almost done?' I asked.

'Yes, I think so. I've made plenty of food that's now in the freezer.'

'I'll be fine, Mum. Just have a good time. Don't worry about me.'

'You're a good girl. Dad and I never knew when we would go back again. I can't look after you well enough and here you are, giving us the money to go back.' She grew silent and I saw her tears building. Tears of relief, of pending joy, but also sadness.

The next day I drove them to the airport. They lined up along with hundreds of other Vietnamese Australians, checking in box upon box of wrapped gifts for their relatives: discounted chocolate from Woolworths, Panadol, appliances and clothes. For many it would be their first time returning to Vietnam, unaware of how the country had developed while they had been gone. They would still recall the days of rations. In their bags would be humble gifts such as toothpaste, redundant in a rapidly modernising nation.

The Vietnam Airlines flight was full. When it was my family's turn to check in, we held our breath as the luggage was weighed. My mother's efforts had paid off and the weight precisely met the limits. After our McDonald's breakfast meal, a rare family treat that we only seemed to enjoy at Sydney airport, I escorted my parents and Vinh as far as the entrance for passengers to immigration. I fussed a final time.

'Do you have medicine for asthma, indigestion, diarrhoea?'

'Yes, yes,' Mum replied.

When I hugged her, she whispered, 'Thank you.' I squeezed her tightly as I felt my tears accumulate. I waved to them as they disappeared down the corridor.

When my family arrived in Vietnam, they called me to tell me they had arrived safely. I heard the laughs and shouting of my relatives in the background. I smiled, aware of the jubilant reunion they were enjoying.

Not long after they left one day, I was driving home from work on Milperra Road at Revesby, past the oversized dimpled golf ball of Putt Putt mini golf land on the left and wholesale fruit and vegetable grocers on the right, when my mobile phone rang. It was too early for a call from my parents in Vietnam. The number was unfamiliar.

'Hello, Cat Thao speaking.'

'Hi, Cat Thao, this is the president of the United Nations Youth Association of Australia calling. I wanted to let you know you have been selected to represent Australia at the United Nations General Assembly in New York.'

I couldn't speak. I pulled over as the person at the other end of the line told me about the next steps, which would involve the Department of Foreign Affairs. I couldn't imagine what it all meant. I was twenty-four years old at the time and the first Australian from a refugee background and the first from Sydney University to take up the position.

●

Before I left for New York for the fifty-eighth session of the United Nations General Assembly, I travelled around Australia to consult with organisations and young people who were involved with youth policy and development. I met with kids in juvenile detention in Sydney, the youth advisory council of Launceston and arts organisations in Alice Springs. I went to see projects in communities in Central Australia with no running water or electricity and where the Indigenous kids didn't speak English. By the time I arrived in New York and met other representatives from as far afield as Fiji, Sweden and Norway, I realised that whatever the state of development of our respective nations, or the specific housing challenges facing various communities or addiction problems facing individuals, any development plan had to address the same issues of participation, representation and ownership. This was the common desire for all of us, wherever we came from in the world.

By the time I left for New York, David and I had drifted apart. We had tried to reconnect but one fundamental obstacle stood in our way: I had changed. I had engaged in activism on all sorts of levels and the relationship between David and I felt stifling. I was going from human rights presentations in Canberra to watching his friends play the poker machines at Mounties. Our connection had frayed; we were no longer bound by common experiences. I yearned for our relationship to be restored somehow but I knew that love alone wasn't enough. We would separate and then get back together again, alternating between irritable conversation and silence. I was fighting for my own sense of self and place. He struggled with trying to understand a girl masquerading as a woman, on the cusp of knowing herself. It was as though years of responsibility and nursing refugee parents with broken English and naivety about Australian society, had smothered my opportunity to develop through a conventional adolescence. Finally, it seemed that the teenage angst of confusion, questions of womanhood and anxious identity dawned upon a girl of twenty-four years of age. Through all my years of turbulence, David had remained steady, loving me with his strength and stoicism. But now I needed to leave.

We said goodbye at the airport. I was going to a foreign place alone for the first time in my life. I was scared of the adventure ahead. Scared of being small and of being great. We held each other tightly through tears until it was time for me to board my flight. I let go of him, my protector, for the last time.

•

I wanted to arrive in New York City a few weeks before starting work to settle in, but I knew no one and essentially had no money. My parents' close friend was part of an alumni network of the National Department of Administration of the Republic of South Vietnam. This department of elite and talented public servants maintained a robust global network, and my parents' friend dutifully made enquiries. He found a man living in Queens with his wife and two grandchildren who would be prepared to host me. I found a cab at JFK airport and gave the driver the address. I gaped out the window as we drove. Everything around me seemed larger than life. The coffee cups were bigger, the people walked taller and the buildings were shinier.

Although the family didn't have much space, they were incredibly generous. One of the granddaughters, who was fourteen years old, was a superb dancer. No sooner had I dumped my luggage in one of their storerooms than I was requested to go to the basement for a performance. With her New York accent, she reminded me of a character from a Woody Allen movie. I watched her dance, dressed in tight white lycra, while her little sister and grandmother glowed with pride.

Later, just before I officially started at the Australian Mission, I moved into an apartment near the corner of Fifty-first Street and First Avenue, just down the road from the Australian ambassador's residence and not far from the United Nations headquarters. As I walked to the Australian Mission opposite the Chrysler building that first day, clutching a bagel I had bought from a street vendor, my spirits soared. (I had ordered a sultana bagel not knowing the Americans called them raisins and the vendor, confused by my Australian accent, had given me one with 'salt-arn-it'.) The glittering grandeur of New York City unfolded before me. The pavements were crowded with New Yorkers power-walking down the street with a coffee in one hand and the paper in the other. Skyscrapers and yellow cabs dazzled me as I walked along. I felt so small in the enormity, diversity and wonder of the city. It was indeed an adventure.

•

The United Nations building was buzzing with activity. Press conferences, Security Council meetings, negotiations. It was like a Hollywood set. The North Korean diplomat was always lodging formal protests at the Special Rapporteur on Human Rights when the country wasn't addressed as the Democratic People's Republic of Korea. The spectacular cafeteria served delicious food from all over the world, and customers were charged by weight under subsidised arrangements. With my red diplomatic pass, I was able to get free tickets to plays, symphonies and stage shows in special concessions offered by the city to diplomats and United Nations staff.

On behalf of Australia, I negotiated a resolution which was passed at the Third Committee of the UN General Assembly. I was the only youth representative at the UN who was allowed to directly negotiate a resolution on behalf of my country like a regular diplomat. I worked with the Portugal delegate and UN Secretariat through the duration of the General Assembly.

The day came when the resolution was to be voted on. I saw the green, red and amber lights come on next to each country's name on a large board. Eventually the resolution was passed and would be implemented in the following year. I was asked to deliver a statement to the General Assembly. From my position behind the Australia seat, I addressed the delegates and the chair. My speech was meant to be delivered after the US and before Cuba. But the US ambassador to the Economic and Social Council came in late and arrived during my speech. He wore a stylish blue suit and had a confident stride. I was to learn that he had come to America as a Cambodian refugee and started off driving taxis. Despite his being decades my senior, we both acknowledged our humble beginnings and celebrated our crossing of paths at this global interchange. Immediately after my speech, he congratulated me in his own statement to the General Assembly. When the session was over he invited me to a karaoke party at the US Mission which I had no hesitation in accepting. Later, we would develop a good rapport and he would invite me to events of interest like off-Broadway shows about refugees. I wondered whether he felt the same as I did at events such as lunch at the Australian Ambassador's residence, where the only people who looked like me often were the serving staff. Still, his presence humbled and reassured me.

I walked down the street towards the United States Mission to the United Nations to attend the karaoke party. The light was fading quickly together with the heat of the day. I passed through several security checkpoints before I was finally admitted to the party. There were about a hundred delegates from various countries. The cocktails had not yet flowed sufficiently when the ambassador grabbed the microphone and invited the Norwegian delegate to perform. She bellowed a version of 'I Will Survive' and we all applauded politely. Then the ambassador asked for the Australian delegate. My ears burned and I tried to hide behind a large European delegate, but it was too late, the ambassador had seen me. He pointed a finger in my direction And the gaze of the room shifted to me, the lights suddenly frying me. I moved towards the stage reluctantly and requested the first song that came into my head—Michael Jackson's 'Beat It'. Because I can't sing very well, I then proceeded to rap the entire song, accompanying my rendition with pathetic moon-walking and crotch-grabbing motions. Moderate applause and chuckles followed as I tried to swiftly disappear into the audience. The US ambassador laughed out loud.

After the performance, I went to the bar to get a much-needed drink. The bartender congratulated me on my performance. We got talking and he asked whether he could show me New York. I thought, 'How lovely New Yorkers are!' He was a former Armani model trying to get more gigs and meanwhile moonlighted as a waiter for a catering company.

We made arrangements and one evening he took me first to a typical New York diner for dinner, and then to see *Rent*, my first-ever Broadway musical. There is no greater magic than the melodrama of people singing on stage with a live band. I couldn't stop beaming and had to consciously prevent myself from squealing like a child. At the end of the evening, he walked me back to my apartment and asked to come in. He then produced a jar of Vegemite in case I was missing home. He also brought out a bottle of wine. I was so naive that I hadn't even realised it was a date. It only occurred to me when he said, 'You look really beautiful tonight.'

'Really?' I must have had a very confused look on my face.

As I was pondering how to respond, he whispered, 'I really want to kiss you.'

'Really?' I said again, baffled, followed by, 'Um, no, sorry. I don't think so. Thanks, though.' I then ushered a very bewildered man out the door of my apartment.

As I began to close the door, he said, 'You really do look beautiful tonight.'

'Um, yeah. Thanks. Good night.' I stood there looking at the Vegemite jar, feeling very awkward. I had met David six years earlier straight out of high school and never really dated. I couldn't even read the standard signs of dating. I was on my own and was in a whole new world that existed and went on without me. I thought about the subtext lining my adventure, a yearning for the comfort of familiarity. I missed David.

New York was a time of learning and tantalising new experiences. That year I saw snow for the first time. I discovered bagels, went to the famed Hammerstein Ballroom and attended hip-hop shows and feminist poetry readings in the East Village. I went to Columbia University to hear lectures by great thinkers whose work I had studied at university, including Noam Chomsky, Milton Friedman and Nobel Prize-winning economist, Amartya Sen. I witnessed how big decisions were made—big decisions that affect little people, like me and my family. I discovered how truly interdependent everything is. I discovered that beyond my family, beyond Bankstown, there was just so much world. And it enchanted me.

•

When I came back to Australia several months later, I craved the same sense of independence I'd had when I lived alone in New York. Close to the beginning of the academic year, I moved out. In my parents' eyes, unmarried Vietnamese women who moved out of home were gangster girls, pregnant or those who had nothing left to hope for. But I sold the idea to them by asserting that since it was my final year of study, I had to concentrate very hard. Hoping that I would finally graduate from law after two deferments, they gave in. In normal circumstances this would have rendered me an unforgivable sinner. So I was not to inform any of our relatives; they would assume that something was wrong.

Clutching my collection of Hitchcock and *Astro Boy* DVDs, I moved into a share house in Enmore, a mere eight minutes by bus from Sydney University's main campus. I lived with three other students—an international student from Nepal, a physics major who was a member of a Gregorian choir and a gay activist of Chinese-Cambodian descent. It was a classic student house, a time of cooking pad Thai, hanging out at the pub on the corner and waking up on Sunday mornings to find my mother downstairs with a box of spring rolls. I wore corduroy pants, bandanas and ate discounted pub meals. I walked up and down the streets of nearby Newtown, browsing through vintage furniture stores and checking out Mexican eateries. It was the student life I had seen on American TV shows and I relished it. However, I could not escape the feelings of guilt that I had abandoned Vinh and my parents. I was living a colourful life away from them. I felt that my freedom and new experiences were at their expense. They could certainly use the money I spent living away from home. Vinh was still in high school and I wasn't there for him. Each day I tried to escape these thoughts, choosing instead to focus on café lattes, used books and live music. But they intruded every so often as I gazed at a schooner of beer or stared out my bedroom window.

Despite the demands on my time made by law school, I returned to my old patterns of diverting my attention to other activities. I continued to serve on the national advisory committee to SBS and the management committee of the Ethnic Communities' Council of New South Wales, while also undertaking an intensive ten-month social leadership program with the Benevolent Society. After returning from the UN, I also travelled around Australia on a national speaking tour. I was a member of the NGO delegation to the UN Committee on the Rights of the Child in Geneva while still working as a project consultant.

As I kept busy with policy work, I found myself in rather interesting circumstances. On one occasion I dined at the New South Wales Governor's residence with Princess Mary and Crown Prince Frederik of Denmark. I decided to wear a traditional Vietnamese dress. A man dressed in an amazing uniform with medals and a sword announced me to their royal highnesses. There were only about forty people at the dinner. Princess Mary was beautiful and Crown Prince Frederik was actually quite laidback. The residence was stunning, looking out over Sydney Harbour, surrounded by meticulously kept gardens. Despite the grandeur, I was too stressed about the array of cutlery to fully appreciate the fabulousness of the occasion. I had never seen so much cutlery and crockery at one meal in my life. Each plate and knife glistened with a gold rim and a crest. I pretended to enjoy my dinner while secretly petrified I would chew too loudly. Each time a new course was served, I stealthily watched what the other guests did with the cutlery and mimicked them while trying to look nonchalant. I tried hard to conceal the pressure I felt by nodding politely at the conversation. Finally, when the night ended, I made my way up the long driveway, shaded by giant trees, to catch a bus back to my shabby share house in Enmore, where I slept on a futon I'd borrowed from my Cambodian housemate.

On another occasion, I was invited to speak at an Australian Chinese association dinner. It was a large dinner and I needed the support of my Cambodian housemate, so he accompanied me. The day of the dinner, he fussed over me and over some hours we workshopped what I would wear. He spray tanned my legs. On my left at the dinner was Kim Beazley, the federal leader of the opposition at the time and the only other speaker that evening. On my right was Justice Marcus Einfeld, a federal court judge, who a few years later would be imprisoned for perjury and attempting to pervert the course of justice. On the table next to me was Senator Penny Wong, who would become the first Asian-born and openly lesbian member of an Australian cabinet.

I was wearing my $5 fake diamond drop earrings. When I had bought them, there was round piece of clear plastic at the back. I didn't realise I was supposed to remove this before wearing them. At my dinner table was also the managing director of one of the largest jewellery companies in Sydney. After I gave my speech and sat down, the guests at my table congratulated me. At the end of the evening, the managing director approached me and gave me his card. 'Any time you have an event where you need to borrow jewellery, you just let me know.' My housemate stared at my plastic and fake diamond earrings. My cheeks flushed with awkward embarrassment as I nodded and thanked him.

The community dinner was not complete without a raffle. The opposition leader gave me his raffle tickets, and to my delight I won. It was a year's supply of fresh juice! My housemate and I were beside ourselves with glee.

Law school was still as stifling as before, but this time I had a couple of allies. I met a brilliant professor of migration law. She was married to the Dean of the Law School at the time, who was a fiercely intelligent blind professor. She advocated for refugees and spoke about them with the deepest humanity. Her conviction was extraordinary and her sense of compassion and dedication to social justice motivated me to forge ahead. In between Intellectual Property, Media Law and Litigation, her classes became a beacon of inspiration and a sacred haven.

Another ally was Brendan. I met him in one of my first Media Law classes. He had shoulder-length curly brown hair and wore the kind of square surf bag that only year five kids carried. I had on my usual headscarf, revealing bits of the platinum blonde streaks my Bankstown train station hairdresser had given me. I recalled Brendan's face from a tutorial I'd attended when I was in first year with Peter. But despite being in the same course, I hadn't seen him again in the intervening five years.

When he called me out of the blue, I didn't even know who he was, even after he told me his name. But I quickly discovered he wasn't like everyone else. While at college, he would catch the train to Cabramatta on weekends to get sugarcane juice. His mates thought he was 'eccentric'. He had taken a year off to travel, which was why he hadn't finished his degree sooner. I came to realise that Brendan saw poetry in the same things I did. In the beauty of a floating leaf, the hidden messages in a song and the struggle to make the world a better place. His political conscience and worldview were cultivated not only by wise and socially aware parents but by confident and intelligent older sisters.

Ours was a slow courtship as, after a game of pool, I dismissed the idea that he could possibly be interested in me. Like his father before him, he had attended The King's School, one of the most elite private schools in Australia. After high school he lived on campus at Sydney University at another elite establishment, St Paul's College.

One evening we walked through Hyde Park, with the fairy lights scattered among the trees and the sun fast descending. We saw rays of light nimbly moving across the cold grass. We decided to chase the sun wherever it would take us. In every patch of light, we lay on the grass holding hands with the world dissolving around us as we remained protected by a halo of love.

Brendan and I devised escapades that helped me to endure the rest of my time in law school. It seemed he was friends with everyone. I always felt uncomfortable when he introduced me to peers who didn't even know I was enrolled there, despite the fact that there had been a colour photo of me on the noticeboard in the foyer ever since my UN assignment. My portrait had stayed on the noticeboard for months and each time I saw it, I would try to scurry into the lift like a cowering criminal, hoping to not be detected. Once I saw a group of students staring at my picture. One of them said, 'Who's that?' 'Dunno,' the others replied.

The first time I met Brendan's parents was at their house on the South Coast at the foot of a small mountain. It was a picturesque hour-and-a-half drive from Sydney. I was nervous, anticipating an unfamiliar world. Outside the Vietnamese community, I had really only visited the homes of friends who were Greek, Albanian and Lebanese. When I arrived, though, I was greeted with warm smiles. I walked through the house Brendan grew up in, examining the timeline of photos, ribbons and trophies, newspaper clippings and toothless primary school smiles. It was exactly like the homes on family television shows. Images of little Brendan blowing into a trumpet, holding a cricket bat and sitting in a school assembly lingered through the house. As I walked through this beautiful museum, I wondered where my equivalent wall of growth was. Where was my history displayed? I recalled that in my grandfather's house in Vietnam I had seen photos of myself as a child, as a teenager. Pictures my parents had sent over were displayed proudly. Birthdays, visits to the zoo. Our family shrine was there. My continuity was there. Not here.

At Easter lunch in Brendan's lovely house, the good china and silver were used and opera played while we ate. Jokes were told and gentle enquiries about me were made. As I drove back to my parents' home, I cried at the contrast between lunch with Brendan's family and Easter lunch with my parents in our small rented house and the humble food offerings to our ancestral/ Virgin Mary hybrid altar. How could my family ever interact comfortably with Brendan's? Each meeting would be a gracious 'Thank you for accepting us into your country,' which Brendan's parents would probably not know how to respond to unless they could squat on plastic mats and eat roasted pig heads. A flood of impossible images bobbed and drifted in my used car like a dirty oil spill, engulfing my mind. With my indelible angst and non-English-speaking parents, how could my relationship with Brendan ever work?

Brendan's friends were mostly white and had attended private schools. One was a professional cricketer whose girlfriend who was a fashion model. Others were investment bankers, engineers and consultants. One evening we were invited to a dinner party in an exclusive apartment building in Potts Point. It was the first time I was to meet some of his friends. I had never been in such a setting before. The banker cooked tuna steaks. They asked about me and where I was from. When I mentioned Bankstown, one of the girls said people out there had an accent and used phrases like 'Fully sick, bro.' She tried to say the phrase in a Western Sydney accent, but it was a really pathetic attempt. I then volunteered how to say it properly. They all erupted in laughter. 'Yes, that's it!'

That evening I felt I was at a masquerade. I felt I was betraying my heritage and my community by pretending to be part of a society I did not belong in, nor want to. Our worlds were so far apart.

•

Brendan had moved to a share house in Redfern, a two-minute walk to university, after living for some time in Darlinghurst, a trendy area near the city. Shortly after, in December 2005, Sydney experienced its worst-ever manifestation of divisive racism in what became known as the Cronulla Riots. The riots erupted after some tussle on the beach between Anglo-Australians and Australians of Middle Eastern descent. It quickly turned violent, with hordes of youths from all over Sydney congregating to protect mosques after threats of arson were made. Anglo-Australians assumed the symbols of nationalism, draping themselves in the flag and wielding cricket bats. Random cars and people were bashed. It was ugly and terrifying. But as I watched these images beam from the television, I saw in many of the non-Anglo faces and heard in the roaring shaky voices the need for validation. The need for acceptance. How many generations must be born here before we were considered to be part of this country? All around Australia, people like me saw the rage and understood its underlying causes.

I was at Brendan's new place in Redfern, dissecting the incident with him. I spoke of how it felt for these Australians to be told to GO HOME from the country of their birth, and how when Australia was symbolised by cricket bats it only confirmed for many of us that this was not our country. It never would be.

Brendan analysed the event more dispassionately. His point of view was intellectual. It was rational. It was insulting. I stormed out of the house and onto the street where my car was parked. He followed, begging me to get out of the car, arguing that I shouldn't drive in my state.

'You will never know what it is like for people like us!' I screamed at him in the disinterested open air. 'You will never understand what racism is and yet you will decide what will become of us, you will decide everything for us!' I saw him as another expression of oppression.

That night Brendan became the Them to my Us. No matter how hard I tried, I would never be able to forgive him for his privilege. I recalled my father's threat when I was sixteen; he would disown me, he'd said, if I ever dated a white boy. This memory was still attached to me like a lead ankle cuff. Despite my growing independence, I still couldn't bring myself to defy my father; I had not yet told my parents about Brendan.

•

In my last year of law school, I wanted to earn extra money, so I got a part-time job working for the TAB, the leading horse and sports betting company. I worked at the racecourse each Saturday, taking bets. I learned all about Boxed Quinellas and Superfectas. I was placed in a different part of the venue each week. The public area was the most colourful, with pensioners in shorts mingling with brides-to-be on a hen's weekend. Many betters would wait until the last few seconds when they were enlightened with some equine intuition before they placed their bets. Often it would be a mixed string of bets and varying dollar values. But the days would all end the same—girls holding their heels in their hands, some vomiting in the bathroom, some faces drooping with disappointment, others gleeful.

Several times I saw people from law school in the VIP pavilion. The girls were glowing with spray tans, fascinators and glossy game-show smiles. I would always shrink into my coloured uniform vest, the mandatory TAB scarf around my neck soaking up my sweat and humiliation. In those moments, I didn't see it as just a job, but as yet another reminder: Me on the service side and Them drinking from champagne flutes. In the seconds just after the races were over, when the roar of the ravenous crowd had throbbed to a climax and then fizzled, sometimes I daydreamed about attending the races as a spectator—a free agent wearing a lacy dress, poised with a glass of sparkling wine and a perfectly positioned hat. Maybe one day. After law school was over.

In between my relationship with Brendan, various jobs, policy work and class, the clerkship season had come around. Each year the elite law students would vie for placements at the giant and illustrious corporate law firms of Sydney. Usually the placement would guarantee a graduate position. A clerkship at one of the top firms meant admission to yet another exclusive club. Even if they didn't want to be a corporate lawyer, the frenzied formula of competitive selection coerced many students to apply anyway for the chance to don a badge of prestige. I too put in an application and was shocked to find out that I had two interviews. Both were top-five law firms housed in buildings with harbour views and their own catering service. One had awarded me a scholarship and so I reasoned had probably granted me an interview out of a sense of obligation.

I was busy running from a community meeting to one of the interviews and I didn't have a jacket. I had on black pants and a white collared shirt – aka my TAB uniform. On the way to the interview, I decided to drop by Pitt Street Mall in the centre of town to see if I could find anything appropriate. To my relief, I found a decent jacket on sale. With eyes honed from our sweatshop years, I knew immediately it was a cheap polyester blend, but I hoped the interviewers wouldn't be able to tell. Before I went to the interview, I needed to drop by the law school library to return a book before I got fined.

After my hasty purchase I ran into the law school foyer and jabbed at the lift button—my portrait on the noticeboard still staring out at me. As I stepped into the lift, a girl joined me. She looked at me and then said politely, pointing at my armpit, 'Um, excuse me, your tag is still on your jacket.'

I looked down. A bright red SALE tag glared back at me. It was luminescent. Horrified, I tried to conceal my embarrassment by saying casually, 'Oh yeah, thanks, I was wondering if anyone would tell me.'

By the time I got to the interview, I was a dishevelled mess. The interviewer's name was Warwick. I had never come across this as the name of a person before. My friends all had either easy-to-pronounce Christian names or their own ethnic ones. Throughout the interview, I pronounced the silent W in the middle—War-wick—which was how the Vietnamese pronounced Warwick Farm. Only later, when I spoke to Brendan, did I understand why Warwick had winced slightly whenever I said his name.

I hoped I would do better at the interview with the second firm. I met with two of the partners, a man and a woman. The woman seemed nice enough. When it came time for me to ask questions, instead of asking about the firm's strategies to expand into Asia or the number of oil and gas joint ventures it had advised on, I asked, 'If you had chosen a career other than law, what would you have chosen?' I was interested to see what sort of people they were. The man said he might have been a yachtsman because he loved sailing. The woman said, 'Maybe a writer.'

That got me excited. 'What's your favourite book?' I asked.

'There are so many, but I really like *The Unbearable Lightness of Being.*'

'Yes, that's a good one,' I agreed.

Silence.

I thought it had gone well, but I wasn't offered a place at either firm. I was pretty sure that my future lay in social justice anyway. As the final classes drew to a close, I finished my placement at the Refugee Advice and Casework Service as well as the Aboriginal Legal Centre in Redfern. I got a job at the New South Wales Legal Aid Commission, primarily working on criminal appeal cases as well as the Balibo Five inquest. (When Indonesia invaded East Timor in 1975, five Australian journalists who had been based in Balibo were murdered.)

I had some extraordinary experiences. Each day was an adventure. I sought out blood experts, analysed police briefs, dissected six months of surveillance in a conspiracy matter, reviewed case law to mount a defence, wrote memos for clients on their civil law matters, prepared cross-examination questions regarding autopsy reports, and ached at the desperation of those who were born into rape, alcoholism and poverty and now were accused of crimes. More often than not it was almost impossible for them not to become a statistic. As I flicked through criminal records in preparation for sentencing submissions, I realised how so many people became dehumanised in case files and numbers. On one occasion I accompanied a barrister to the psychiatric ward of a maximum-security prison to meet with our client regarding his plea in a grave sexual assault case. Inside the prison, a gallery space contained recycled trauma, pain and mental illness, transformed into artworks. For many other prisoners, despite the art program, their hurt lived on in nightmares and a continuing life of crime. In the taxi ride back to the office, I spoke with the barrister about a variety of things. He was interested in the art. Our conversation meandered between references to the case, to the overall 'Aboriginal Situation' and to fashion. A few years later, I read that he committed suicide. I realised that everyone's pain was relative, only to them.

Brendan became a lawyer before me. He got a job in rural New South Wales as a criminal lawyer. One weekend, we drove the four hours from Sydney to his rented flat in Wagga Wagga. I stayed for a week to help him set up. I bought second-hand furniture at St Vinnies and cooked him Thai, Italian and Vietnamese meals. I walked up and down the main strip trying to find another Asian person. I finally found one working at the ice-cream parlour. Sometimes we ate counter meals at the pub. During the day, I watched *Oprah* and *Dr Phil*. I dressed up, listened to rock music and drank dirty martinis alone like a bored housewife. At night Brendan would bring piles of case files home and we would analyse the evidence like we were in law school again. Classes seemed so far away. But this was real life now. They weren't just the Accused. These were real people. Brendan wrote Spanish poetry for me while we listened to Leonard Cohen. Despite the little world we had created for ourselves, I felt the film of our bubble thinning as the cricket community club beckoned and he was drawn more and more into the life of the country town. Something that I could never fathom being a part of.

•

'What if I married a white person?' I asked my mother one day when I was driving her to go grocery shopping. I hadn't yet told her about Brendan.

There was a contemplative silence as we pulled up at the red light.

'Your father and I have been in this country almost as long as we lived in Vietnam. As long as you are really happy it would be fine.'

'What about Dad?'

'Dad will be okay.'

I felt her disarming sense of grace and was overcome with admiration for my mother's ability to adapt and to change. In that moment, thoughts of Brendan faded as I became overwhelmed with an indescribable love for my mother. I saw the core essence of her being and how we had come to be. As survivors.

CHAPTER 12

An arrival

It was a cool February day. As usual, buses, trucks and modified sports cars thundered past our house on Chapel Road, Bankstown. The volunteers at the Salvation Army store down the street had put out the furniture for sale. Students were waiting at the bus stop several houses down. Inside our house, my family was getting ready. My father put on his only suit, a white collared shirt and the same navy blue tie he wore to weddings, funerals, graduations and major church events. He put on the cufflinks bearing the United Nations logo which I had bought for him at the UN souvenir shop in New York. My mother was dressed in a long-sleeved black shirt with a frenzied disco pattern straight out of the 1980s, charcoal-grey trousers and black sandals. Some part of her ensemble always included items from St Vinnies. I looked at my tired, ageing parents. My father with his hair-sprayed comb-over and greying eyebrows, and my mother, make-up free (as she never learned how to apply it), and in her effort not to look like a peasant, presenting herself to the world as the queen of Western Sydney. This was their Best Dress. This was the day their daughter would become a lawyer.

We parked the car at Bankstown Sports Club then walked to the train station. I noticed my father was still wearing steel-capped heavy shoes from his factory days. He had shrunk visibly in the last few years. His $3 glasses, still with the +2.0 sticker on them, hung defiantly on the wrinkled bridge of his nose.

I had decided that, for the occasion, I was going to buy leather shoes for the first time in my life. I deserved it. My new high heels clicked noisily on the tiles of Bankstown station. A few workers, students and shoppers were clustered around the bottom of the stairs. My parents and I rarely travelled to the city together. The only occasions I could recall were when we had relatives visiting from overseas. We'd take them to town to show them the opera house and harbour bridge from Circular Quay. None of our visitors ever saw *inside* the opera house. We always stood outside on the steps and took photos of the white sails until the visitor complained they were cold—even in summer.

We sat down on the blue benches at the station platform. I wondered about the first time my parents caught a train in this new land, all those decades ago. With a young family and no car, in an effort to save money on groceries, each weekend my parents had pulled a shopping cart across several train lines to reach the wholesale fruit and vegetable market at Flemington.

They became familiar faces to the Vietnamese farmers who brought their produce there with barefoot children clambering under the tables and fighting with each other as their parents struggled to make a living.

The train arrived on time. It was a newer train with air conditioning and fabric seat covers. The sun shined slightly as we began our ride to St James station. It was going to be a good day.

The familiar stations on the Bankstown line rolled past me as they had thousands of times before. So did the landscapes of our life in Australia. We passed Punchbowl station, dotted with the multicultural faces of mothers pushing prams unbalanced by groceries. It was the station where I used to watch the rats weave in and out behind the takeaway store while waiting for a train to my first high school. Punchbowl was where my parents had saved enough money to buy their own piece of Australia. It was where they established a stake of pride which hosted my grandparents' single visit to Australia, only to see our optimism smashed as we lost our home, desperately clinging onto our dignity. I recalled the day we moved into a room in my uncle's rented home and my father's unbearable snoring as all five of us were packed into a bed. It was in that house as a young teenager that I began to comprehend my parents' desperate struggles. I saw the unequivocal urgency and pain in my mother's face as she sewed night and day, even after the death of her mother. I witnessed the anguish of abuse that my father suffered on the factory floor. As a child in that Punchbowl house, I felt abandoned to look after my baby brother whose incessant crying pierced at me as my parents worked hard to deliver the garments. It was in that house that I felt I was truly alone and the world did not let me dream.

We whizzed past Lakemba station. For years I had alighted at that station to attend MacKillop Girls High School every day. We went past King Georges Road and the Cao Đài Holy Temple where my grandmother's death ceremony was held. We passed the street where Văn attended tae kwon do practice. From my seat on the train I could see Lakemba Library. It was there where, at thirteen, I literally ran away towards the station from my first crush after he said a simple 'Hi'. Lakemba station was where I witnessed constant bouts of tension bordering on violence. I recalled the aftermath of the bloody battle between students and their red-stained school uniforms. It seemed like a long-ago, faded memory.

A few stops later we reached Marrickville station. An old man with heavy grocery bags sat waiting on a bench. Marrickville was the first place we settled in properly after our time at the immigration hostel in Villawood. I remembered the flats we'd played around opposite the station. This was where neighbours had taught my mother to sew and from where my father walked every day to work in a factory instead of catching the train, in an effort to save money. The place where we'd had the first Christmas I could recall, with a disappearing Santa and the smell of beer puncturing the air. There was a makeshift manger for Baby Jesus made of discarded brown paper and industrial netting from my uncle's factory. The men would drink and sing and wallow in nostalgia. Marrickville was a time of relief from war but being there brought with it the pressure to navigate our way through a strange new land. It was the place of my first memories: the frightening world of preschool, meeting my moustached uncle and my mother escaping my frantic grasp to go to work.

We pulled into Sydenham station, a major interchange which serves the inner west, Bankstown and eastern suburbs lines. The foot traffic is a mix of working class, students and young professionals. As we pulled into Sydenham station, I saw an Asian girl in a high school uniform sitting alone, waiting for her train. She was small with an oversized bag. She was gazing into the distance, and I was reminded of myself so many years ago, sitting on the same bench. Waiting for the future. A wilderness beyond the imagination of my teenage burdened self. This was also the station where, in my final two years of high school, I had changed trains from Punchbowl for Kogarah to attend St George Girls. Each morning, a few Vietnamese girls and I had met in the third carriage from the end and bantered about school, boys, parents and the formal. Each morning, we got off the train at Sydenham and pulsed up the stairs along with the torrent of alighting passengers. We descended to Platform 6, huddled together in our short skirts, stealing conspicuous glances at the Catholic boys in blazers. Despite our frivolous gossip, the unremitting mantra to pursue academic excellence was silently sung and always hung around us refugee children, like the end notes from a choir.

Those last two years of high school blitzed past me. I was still an awkward girl, unsure and unsteady. I tried with all my might to be the best but before year twelve ended, my shoulders began to droop with the burden of responsibility and familial duty. Knowing my parents had bigger issues to deal with and knowing the world they understood had clear boundaries, I didn't have the solace of sharing with them trivial matters like friendship feuds or how I should tackle school assignments.

As I remembered my teenage self, I was baffled at how I came to be here today, sitting on this train with my beloved parents beside me, on our way to the New South Wales Supreme Court.

As the train slowly pulled away from Sydenham, we could just make out the skyline of the city.

'Mum, can you see Centrepoint Tower?'

'Where?'

'Over there!'

I looked at my mother, straining to see the iconic building. A worn but proud woman who'd spent the most youthful and vibrant years of her life religiously at the sewing machine, hoping that this day would come. A day once so unreachable.

As we passed through St Peters and Erskineville, the houses got smaller and the streets got tighter. New inner-city apartments were being erected for young professionals who all dressed in the same hipster uniform—even on weekends.

We are now arriving at St James station. Suddenly, the old iron railings and vintage advertisements of Arnott's biscuits and NRMA insurance appeared as our train pulled in. The green trim of tile followed the tunnel to the surface like a steady snake. The echoes with the footsteps of business shoes, high heels and aspirations fluttered through the narrowness. St James station: home to Sydney University's law school campus and the historic New South Wales Supreme Court. We walked up the platform and slid our tickets into the machines. My parents hesitated, revealing how unaccustomed they were to train travel. Their Vietnamese voices reverberated in the dull tunnels winding upwards and outwards. We walked through the tunnels, past the sleeping homeless man, and I wondered where Gus, the saxophone player, was today. His sounds had kept me company so often. I recalled his encouraging words when I shared with him how despondent I felt each time I went to law school. He always gently reminded me of simpler things to hold onto and appreciate—how lucky I really was.

We went up the flight of stairs ascending to street level. With each step, the expanse of light became more encompassing. And then there it was. The New South Wales Court emerged before us like a lord from feudal times. Monumental. Regal. The highest court in the state of New South Wales established in the nineteenth century. A symbol of justice, of the people, of democracy. Ideals pursued and held onto by my parents as they left the only country they had ever known.

Across from the court was the law school. I walked my parents through to the law school foyer and showed them where my portrait had hung a couple of years earlier. My father quaintly smiled in appreciation as he crossed his hands behind his back.

He now had an old man's walk. I saw in his stooped posture the years of heavy factory work and the strain of forever being a foreigner in this land where he carried his own muted cries. Vietnam was so far away but somehow I could still see an invisible rope to his ageing mother and his homeland, connected by a collection of pre-war and war-time memories.

'Let's have a coffee at the café next door,' I suggested. It was only on special occasions that my parents ever sat down anywhere and ordered coffee. My father's daily dose of caffeine came from instant granules of Nescafé. As they looked around at the lawyers and legal assistants, my mother was clearly the only one in a speckled disco shirt. I brought the coffee over, I explained the meaning of the funny wigs and gowns to my parents.

My father began his only way of intimate engagement: conversations about pre-unified Vietnam. 'Before 1975 . . .' I listened as my father rambled on about university in the days of President Diem and how Communism had destroyed quality education. I saw the animation in the lines around his mouth and eyes, and the way he leaned in with his good ear when my mother spoke. Dried bits of the cheap hairspray delicately fell onto the shoulders of his suit like flakes of dandruff. I brushed them away and quietly sipped my latte.

Brendan, who was also going to my legal admission, walked into the café, tall and handsome in his suit, his hair shorter now as befitting a lawyer. I had told my parents about Brendan. This was their first meeting. My mother had prepped my father to make sure he would be pleasant. As Brendan shook my father's hand, my mother snapped too many photos. My father smiled excessively. After too much awkward smiling from everyone, I suggested we get ready to go inside the court.

Inside the Supreme Court building, we emptied our pockets onto trays and walked through the security scanners on our way to the Banco Court on level thirteen. Large oil-painted portraits of former judges hung along the walls like watchful ancestors. Inside the Banco Court, my heart began to race as my parents went to nestle in their seats among the audience of family, sponsors and employers while I joined the other soon-to-be lawyers preparing for admission. The Chief Justice entered in full robe. A solemn, ceremonial silence pervaded the room.

Those seeking admission stood up one by one, each accompanied by a practising lawyer. According to the rules of legal admission, only a current member of the profession can endorse your membership. Families beamed and brimmed with pride. A thousand thoughts shot through me. Then it was my turn. My parents watched with revered and proud curiosity as my sponsor and I rose to our feet.

'I, Brendan Michael Alastair Cahill, move Cat Thao Nguyen to be a member of this honourable court.' As we sat down, Brendan slipped me a smile. A heartening smile, so warm and comforting, I struggled to hold back the tears.

You swear or declare and affirm that you will truly and honestly conduct yourself in the practice of a Lawyer of the Supreme Court of New South Wales and that you will faithfully serve as such in the administration of the laws and usages of this State according to the best of your knowledge, skill and ability?

I swear.

The Chief Justice spoke of commitment to contributing to the legal profession. That duty required us to do so by upholding ethics and standards of excellence. I drank in every word. After his speech, I looked around this bastion of the legal fraternity, surrounded by portraits of forbears of the profession. An institution of prominence. I saw myself as an overgrown child in the middle of this prestigious court—an emblem of achievement, arbiter of truth. The sea of faces, young and old, was awash with respect inside this honourable chamber. *I am here.*

Everyone in the court stood up while the bench of judges filed out. As people hurried down the corridor to the lifts, I remained behind with my parents until we were alone outside the Banco Court. My mother, a former law student who was robbed of what I had now become, stood humbly that day—almost swallowed by the imposing carpet of level fourteen. My parents would later tell me that when they'd left Vietnam they never could have dreamed of such a moment: standing inside the Supreme Court of New South Wales as their daughter became a lawyer. I looked at my parents with their constant terrible memories hovering just beneath their skin; I thought of landmines, of wet footprints in Cambodian jungles, of sewing machines, steel-capped boots, boxes of vegetables from wholesale markets and unpaid bills from far, far away, streaking around us like a snake of coloured lights. I saw a young woman huddled in the middle of the night in a rice field close to the Vietnam–Cambodia border, clutching a baby, as gunshots exploded in the dark. I saw a young man inside a barbed-wire compound, separated from his wife, ready to take his own life. And now they stood before me.

I sobbed into my father's shoulder as he patted my back. All I could say was a muffled, 'Thank you.'

It had been a long and turbulent journey. The three of us held each other awkwardly; it was a rare moment of physical affection that I relished. I longed for us to be like that forever. We stayed like that for a long time, none of us knowing what to say, how to express all that we felt: that this was an arrival at a destination that for so long our hearts and souls had humbly hoped for, had silently suffered for, barely having enough courage to dream it would come true.

As my mother finally pulled away, she squeezed my hand. She softly smiled through her tears as the staff ushered us towards the lifts. *We are here.*

Acknowledgements

This book was written to honour my family, especially my parents. I am indebted to them for demonstrating and teaching me grace, humility, courage and dignity. I thank my brother Văn for paving the way and my brother Vinh for his unrelenting wisdom and belief in me. To my cousin Hải, I wish you peace. To my patient husband, Tony, thank you for being my source of strength and allowing me to be vulnerable. I thank my best friend, Caroline, a true sister who through the most difficult times is my lighthouse. To Chris Butler, thank you for your faith and occasional wit. To Oliver Phommavanh for first demonstrating all is possible. There are many people mentioned in the book who played an integral role in my life. They have healed me, transformed me and helped me to come closer to myself. To these people, I thank you and wish you true happiness.

I am so grateful to the team at Allen & Unwin for their support, especially for the efforts and insights of Annette Barlow, Siobhán Cantrill and Ali Lavau. I would especially like to thank Richard Walsh, who in 2007 read an article in the *Sydney Morning Herald* and with great clarity saw a woman with a story to tell. Over six years, Richard encouraged and worked with me. Thank you deeply, Richard, for your vision and your illuminating conversations.

To my uncle, Hồng Khanh, who disappeared somewhere in Cambodia—may your spirit rest in peace as you watch over us. To all the unnamed people who helped us leave Vietnam, especially the French-speaking Cambodian man whose sarong I hold as I write this, you delivered my mother to safety. Without your compassion, I would not be. Wherever you are, thank you. Finally, we are grateful to the numerous others who assisted us to settle in Australia and gave us hope—whether a smile, a black-and-white television or a phone to call home, we cannot forget the kindness of strangers. May we hold onto a sense of humanity and remember the power of a simple gesture of kindness.